Reading Between The Lines Of Company Accounts

D1637745

Reading Between The Lines Of Company Accounts

by

Stephen Bloomfield

RIGHT WAY
plus

Typeset in 11/12 pt Legacy Serif Book by Letterpart Ltd., Reigate, Surrey.

Printed and bound in Great Britain by Guernsey Press Co. Ltd., Guernsey, Channel Islands.

The *Right Way Plus* series is published by Elliot Right Way Books, Brighton Road, Lower Kingswood, Tadworth, Surrey, KT20 6TD, U.K. For information about our company and the other books we publish, visit our website at www.right-way.co.uk

Contents

Dedication

To PEB and KEB

Section One

Chapter 1:

Introduction . . . and some small print!

How *not* to make Financial Decisions

Lots of investment decisions about precious nest eggs are made on very little knowledge, where no outside analysis exists, based only on guesswork (which may be misleading); on rumour (which may be mistaken); on hunches (which may be unfounded); or on the supposed reputation of a friend or newspaper tipster (who may have been lucky once).

All too often this sort of decision about companies in which to invest proves to be inadequate. Only a little extra knowledge of what accounts are, what they mean and what they can (and cannot) tell you, might help illuminate some darker corners and make those nest eggs a little bit less likely to get scrambled.

This book is intended to provide that knowledge and help a range of readers who may be interested in looking at a company report and accounts for a variety of reasons but who have no formal training in accountancy or book-keeping. It does not assume any detailed prior knowledge of accounts as such, or even of accounting principles, but it does assume some everyday familiarity with basic concepts like profit and loss, debt and credit and the distinction between assets and liabilities.

It will be helpful if the reader has access to a set of accounts (or better still to a run of these over three or four years) of a business (large or small), against which an understanding of the ideas and suggestions that are developed in the text can be tested in practical terms.

Structure of the Book

The book is organised into three broad sections:

The **first section** (Chapters 1 to 6) deals with fundamentals, and both the organisation of the information and the mental approach necessary to begin analysing accounts.

The **second section** (Chapters 7 to 14) deals with the detail of the numbers tabulated in the three 'legs' of the accounts themselves – the Profit and Loss account, the Balance Sheet and the Sources and Uses of Funds Statement – so that you become familiar with the concepts involved in preparing them. This will provide an understanding of what goes on behind the preparation of the numbers.

The **final section** (Chapters 15 to 24) deals with the detail of the accounts in an applied way. The purpose of this section is to combine the information learned in the first two sections to produce a working ability to break down and analyse a set of accounts. In particular, it tries to restore to the accounts some of the time component that is inevitably flattened out in the summarising of the events of a year into a table of numbers spread across one or two pages.

The restoration of this time dimension is a very important point to grasp. **The key to understanding accounts in a dynamic fashion is seeing the numbers, not just as a slab of data, but as a strip of information that runs through a period of time.**

Words of Warning

First, a general warning about what this book can and cannot do: the techniques which are dealt with in these pages have to be supplemented with information from many other sources in order to gain a complete and rounded picture of how a business is doing. There is only room in this book to touch on some of the information supplementary to the accounts which can be used to gain a wider insight into a business's affairs. You will probably discover sources of your own as you investigate the subject further.

Second, while an understanding of the techniques that are outlined in this book will give an insight into how to break down a set of accounts to show things that are not immediately apparent on the surface, this book will not itself produce a fully-fledged Sherlock Holmes of accounts – no matter how carefully the techniques are read or how diligently applied. Analysing accounts, to make them reveal information that the authors did not really want them to, takes quite a lot of practice – more than can be gained just from reading one book like this.

Third, if you look at the fine print of a set of accounts you will see a disclaimer about the 'true and fair view' that the accounts represent. This is signed and, most importantly, *dated* by the auditors. Accountants will tell you that this is a health warning for the users of the accounts. But since the writing is usually small and is tucked away in the boring bit that precedes the numbers (even more boring for most people?) that claim is open to some criticism.

It really would be much better if every set of accounts carried a health warning in big bold letters to the effect that the information contained therein is:

1)   Unreliable
2)   Full of mistakes
3)   Prepared by people who are sloppy, poor record keepers and prone to forgetting things (although no more than normally so) and
4)   More than occasionally deliberately designed to mislead or obscure the truth.

Many sets of accounts are like that, in at least one respect, as we shall see. And *most* sets of accounts can be criticised for at least one of those characteristics!

Types of Accounts Covered

Wherever possible, I have tried to maintain a neutrality between the types of business that might be investigated. The techniques which I have described should work for any type of enterprise, whether sole trader, small limited company or PLC.

However, it is very difficult, without being unduly repetitive, always to use the same descriptive titles; so the reader may well find that occasionally the terms 'business' or 'company' are being used when what he (or she) might want to know about is partnerships or sole-trading accounts. Don't be put off by the apparent focus of these terms; the techniques apply to all the types of organisation that will be found and no concentration is intended on any one commercial type. However, in doing very detailed work on a set of accounts you may have to be aware of the particular legal characteristics of the trading type that you are interested in and if you need to know the details of this then you should consult one of the many specialist texts on the legal aspects of incorporation, sole trading and partnerships.

Although much of the ground that this book covers will deal with the analysis of trends behind published figures, which is a primary technique of investment analysts and stockbrokers, what the book is *not* intended to be is a guide to investing in the sense of where to put your money or how to invest in stocks and shares.

So Who Might Find this Book Useful?

All that having been said, there are a couple of obvious categories of people who are likely to find this book of use.

First, it may be of help to those who do wish to invest – or already have an investment – in smaller companies. Even if these are listed on a Stock Exchange they are usually not well covered by brokers' reports, newspaper columnists or financial journals.

Second, the active investor might want to use the techniques described in the book to check the assessments of (usually) larger companies that can be obtained from tip-sheets, newspapers or the huge range of financial journals – some long-lived, some less so – that are commonly available. The standards (technical and moral) of financial journalism are very variable and, while long-standing newsletters are likely to be very good, it has been known for tips to be given for the most unsavoury of reasons – as cases involving share tipsters and their editors in major national newspapers have shown.

So, within this category, the beneficiaries of legacies, managers of investment clubs or people inheriting small portfolios of shares in private companies might find it useful to conduct their own research – rather than simply turn the task over to someone else whose price for doing it might be disproportionately high in relation to the value involved – or rely on the 'advice' of someone who may have a very personal reason for wanting a share to move in a certain direction.

Third, businessmen about to supply to, or buy from, other businesses may find it useful in helping to reveal some of the features of a potential trading partner's affairs that are not ordinarily visible from a simple examination of accounts. Many businesses are only too happy to accept business from others without some form of reference – some may even sub-contract work without a full knowledge of their sub-contractors' financial strength. This is a strange attitude to adopt since the results of not knowing about your competitors', suppliers' and partners' financial position can, on occasion, be very costly.

These categories of reader will all have different requirements in terms of the amount of information they wish to draw from an examination of published accounts. But, whatever their needs, a word of caution must be sounded at the outset. No matter how good the technical quality of the analysis that is performed, it will only reveal *patterns* in the information that is used. *Since financial information is almost never real-time almost any information will, by definition, be out of date.* So the patterns that you find might not have existed beyond the time covered by the report and accounts at which you have been looking.

A Financial Health Warning

No matter how confident you are of your improved ability to analyse a set of accounts after reading this book, I suggest that you try out some of your new skills by practising with dummy runs first. This is a particularly good idea if you are going to be risking money in investments. You might like to try giving yourself a notional pot of cash and constructing a portfolio for yourself, so that you can track some share prices over a period of time to see if your analyses would have borne fruit if you had backed them with real cash. (You can go to websites like Motley Fool – www.fool.co.uk – to set up an automated tracking system that takes all the hard work out of calculating share prices and portfolio values). Supplement your own analyses with wide-ranging reading to find out the opinion of other commentators about the sectors you are interested in, or about general economic circumstances that affect the companies or businesses which you have selected.

The techniques that are described in this book are a guide to understanding some of the further reaches of companies' accounts so that they tell their story more truthfully and more openly. The reader will have been alerted to some of the tricks, deliberate or inadvertent, that arise in preparing accounts. Nonetheless, the techniques of analysis are not an infallible tool to predict exactly what is going to happen inside a business.

You have been warned!

Chapter 2:

The Language of Accounts

---

*The twin meanings of the word 'accounts'
*Combining these so they tell a story
*The language of accounts

When the word 'account' is used in conversation it probably conjures up in most people's minds one of two things: either a set of numbers spread across (or perhaps down) a page that looks very complicated; or the story of a sequence of events. The two meanings will probably be distinctly different to most people.

But what we are going to do in this book is to let a set of company financial statements combine those two meanings. If we know where to look and without too much effort, the accounts (in the first sense of the word) will tell us an account (in the second sense of the word).

Like all stories, though, unless it is told in a language that you can understand, it won't mean very much to you.

So we shall have to begin this book by learning the vocabulary of the tale that we are going to let the accounts tell us. This means that we shall have to spend some time describing, very simply, some of the basic concepts that have to be grasped before any adventurous analysis can be started.

This will involve three fairly simple sections beginning with Chapter 7 and ending with Chapter 13 – one on each of the three legs of the accounting tripod: the Profit and Loss account; the Balance Sheet; and the Sources and Uses of Funds Statement (the first and last of these are often abbreviated to P&L and S&U). These chapters will ensure that you understand, from the start, the terms that are going to become familiar as you go on to look at the detail of the story the accounts will tell.

Once you have done that, you can look at how to get the accounts to tell their story – in all its detail. This will require much more than simply looking at the numbers – but, unfortunately, there is no getting round the need to understand the basics of accounts and some of the specialised terms that are used in dealing with the numbers.

Each time we return to the three components of accounts we shall explore a bit deeper so that when you come to look at them in practice they gradually reveal more and more of their story.

There are plenty of technical books to tell you in greater or lesser degrees of complexity just what accounts are, how they are compiled and how they are to be used for measuring and recording activity. We are less concerned in this book with that side of accounts and more with the practical usage of the information contained in the accounts. What most people who pick up this book will want to know is how to go about *the process of using accounts for some purpose*. So we shall concern ourselves mostly with practice and not too much theory.

But first we should begin with getting you to think like an analyst.

Chapter 3:

Thinking Like an Analyst

The basic tool of analysis – comparison
Jigsaws
Thinking systematically
Putting the target in context
Local knowledge and some basic economics
Example of simple, practical research
*The need to think around the operational background of a
  company*

The majority of the work in analysing accounts involves comparing information. The information you will use will be harvested from:

1) Within the same year's set of accounts of the company in which you are interested;
2) Previous years' accounts from the same company;
3) Accounts of other companies in the same business from both the same year as you are looking at and from previous years.

You are going to build up a picture of the operations of the business in the same way that you build a jigsaw puzzle – by looking at individual pieces of information; turning them over; seeing if they fit with what you already have; and gradually making the picture larger. Like a jigsaw puzzle, you are never going to force the pieces into place – if you have to do that, you've got the wrong piece of puzzle!

One of the things that you must grasp from the very start

is that you are going to try to restore some of the dimension of time to the accounts. Published accounts 'flatten' the information that they describe by removing the effects of time. Any report does that, of course, unless it takes the same length of time as the original event (in which case there is no point in having it!). You are going to 'unflatten' the accounts slightly so that you can see a little better some of the things that went on in the period you are looking at and put some of the time component back into the picture. This is very important in getting a grasp of how things developed.

Part of this process will be getting your ways of thinking into tune with the accounts.

And here I need to go on a bit of a digression. Quite simply, it is best if you have some idea of the industry, trade or business of the company you are about to analyse, so that you don't have to think too much out of the frame in which the accounts are placed. You need to put the accounts into a context.

Most people who are interested enough in the subject to have picked up this book in the first place will probably have some basic knowledge of the structure of the national economy; the structure of the local economy in the region in which they live; and probably of some of the local industry. That will probably be sufficient – for the purposes of simple analysis – in understanding the background to the company's operations.

Everyday economics – the sort that you pick up through experience, not the sort that you have to be taught – will be sufficient to guide you through understanding the complexities of a simple business's operational environment, *provided that you are willing to think about that background in a reasonably systematic way.*

In the past, when the national economy was less sophisticated, regional specialisations were very much more apparent. Crudely, for England and Wales, heavy industry was congregated in the north east of the country; light and precision engineering around the Midlands; extractive industry in Wales; farming in East Anglia. Scotland had its own regional specialisations.

Clear-cut regional economic distinctions fell away after the Second World War and most people now live in a local economy which is a mix of commercial offices, market gardening, some light engineering and retail-based businesses. The UK economy has moved away from the primary (extractive) industries through the secondary (manufacturing) sector and into the tertiary (service) economy as it has grown and developed.

However, it is probably still the case that the prosperity of the area in which you live is largely dictated by the fortunes of one or two large employers or of a local specialised industry.

So the first thing to do is to try to set your existing knowledge and experience in motion and to order it to serve your purpose in looking at the background to the company or business you want to analyse.

For instance, if you come from Newcastle-upon-Tyne, you probably have a bit of practical knowledge of the economics of the heavy engineering industry. Or, if you come from Stoke or Stafford, the chances are you know what affects prosperity in the pottery and fine china industry. If you come from the Midlands you will probably know a bit about the precision engineering and brick-making industries – even though you may not think you do.

If you genuinely don't know anything about the industry then you could do worse than to pick up a serious newspaper and try to pick out the items of financial and business news that might have an impact on your chosen industry.

Or, perhaps, you can do some practical research, too. For instance, let's say that you are interested in a light engineering company owned by a friend who has asked you if you would like to buy in and become a shareholder, since he has a big project coming up and needs some help in the business. You pass by the local job centre on your way from your office to the sandwich shop each lunch-time and so you decide to drop in one day and look at the jobs on offer. You find that there are lots of offers of jobs for skilled machinists which have been unfilled for several weeks. What does that mean for your friend's firm? For example, will it be able to complete the large contracts it has on hand unless it is able to pay higher wages to keep its staff (because, if skills are in short supply, other employers may well try to poach staff away)?

Or perhaps you are interested in some shares in a housebuilding firm that an aged aunt left to you in her will. The day after you receive the shares, the first paper that you pick up says, in big headlines splashed across the front page, that the mortgage rate is going up. Have a guess about how that's going to affect housebuilding!

If you own a house – or even if you do not – you will know that higher interest rates mean higher mortgages which means people have less money to spend on other things. This may mean that some people will not be able to afford the higher payments that will come from increasing their mortgages to buy bigger houses – or that those wanting to buy new houses might find that their incomes are now insufficient.

So, housebuilders don't like increased mortgage rates and the general belief is that housebuilding companies' share prices suffer when interest rates go up.

The first thing to do, then, is to **think around** the business that you are interested in to see if you can **set it in context**. If you don't do that then you are going to make your job of analysis much harder, because you won't have any reference points. It doesn't matter if those reference points have to be changed later; just for now set down some markers in your own mind about what you *think* you might find.

Chapter 4:

The Contents of a Report and Accounts

The differences between types of accounts
What a typical company report contains

All businesses are required – one way or another – to produce statements of their profits. Limited companies have a statutory obligation to prepare and publish them, in a certain way, for their shareholders, while partnerships and sole-traders have to produce them (though generally in a less formal way) for the purposes of income tax assessment.

Before you even start to have a look at what a set of accounts is, or shows us, or what it can do, you need to think about accounts in a certain way.

Probably the best way to describe that process of thinking is to show you what an analyst would come across as he leafs through a set of accounts for the first time.

This chapter and the next will take you through the format of a normal set of accounts and introduce you to some of the things of which you might take note.

Since we are going to be talking about various types of accounts in some detail, one of the first distinctions that has to be made is between 'Statutory' Accounts and other types – which are usually called 'Management' accounts.

Definitions:

Statutory Accounts are the accounts which companies must prepare by law. In the UK they are the accounts which companies (and only companies) registered in England and Wales must present to the Registrar of Companies each year, within a certain time limit, in a format dictated by the Companies' Acts. Once presented to the Registrar the accounts are public documents. (There is a very similar arrangement in Scotland and Northern Ireland, and other territories and jurisdictions worldwide will have similar requirements.)

Management accounts are the accounts prepared by the management of a business (any sort of business – sole trader, partnership or limited company) to enable them to control the business. They can be in any format that the management choose and are regulated (as far as companies only are concerned) simply by the general requirement to keep proper books of account. They are not publicly available documents.

Let's describe a typical set of Statutory Accounts that you might pick up, so that you are familiar with what they contain. Most of the detail which is set out here relates to accounts published by Public Limited Companies (PLCs), whose shares are traded on the London Stock Exchange – but the format will be essentially the same for all companies, since it is regulated by law. However, private companies usually display less information in their accounts than larger companies because they are not subject to the additional, comprehensive, publication requirements of **listing**, which is the term for having your shares placed on the Stock Exchange's 'Official List' of traded shares.

So, in looking at a set of accounts for a PLC, probably the first information that you will find will be . . .

The Financial Highlights

This is usually a brief graphical representation of what happened during the year to the company. It employs a technique that we are going to use extensively – *direct comparison of one year's information with that of another.*

After that (or, if the company is privately owned, probably first of all) will come . . .

The Chairman's Statement

This is an opportunity for the chairman to sum up to the company's shareholders what has gone on during the year, highlighting significant events – entries into new markets, acquisitions, disposals, general trading performance – and sometimes it contains details of what the company expects for the forthcoming year.

Tucked around the beginning of the set of accounts – perhaps even on the inside front or back covers – will be a list of the companies in which the 'parent company' of the group (if it is a group that you are looking at) has 'an interest'. This interest can range between ownership (which, for accounting purposes, is between 50 and 100 per cent – in which case the company is a subsidiary or joint venture); associate status (26 to 49 per cent) and a trade investment (less than 26 per cent).

This is usually followed by . . .

Directors and Advisers

This is a list of the major advisers to the company – accountants/auditors; solicitors; bankers – and, often, brief biographical details of the members of the board of directors of the company to accompany their names.

Then comes . . .

The Review of Operations

This is where you will find much of value in helping you with background details about the company. It often breaks activities down into divisional reports so that you will be able to find out about progress on – perhaps – individual contracts or markets and describes specific events that have a bearing on the numbers in the accounts. This section is usually written by the managing directors of the subsidiary companies (if there is a group structure) or by divisional heads. The Review is a very valuable section but is not usually found in the accounts of private companies – for the very good reason that it reveals so much about the business. The London Stock Exchange has decreed that investors and shareholders should have access to this information to enable them to make informed decisions about their investments but private company shareholders might not want this degree of detail revealed.

After the Review of Operations comes . . .

The Financial Review

This again is usually limited to the accounts of listed companies. This section complements the operational review by giving details of the major financial events of the year and will again contain lots of comparative information.

After all this has been provided, listed companies will usually give details of the remuneration of their directors and employees, with details about directors' shareholdings, options, and any share dealing that took place during the year.

There is also a separate and obligatory **Directors' Report** which describes the way that the company is managed according to the Companies' Acts (the technical term for this is 'corporate governance') and which also gives references to other items which are usually dealt with elsewhere in considerable detail. Major shareholdings held by outsiders also have to be disclosed in this section.

Only once all these are out of the way does the company get down to the 'meat' of the accounts – the actual numbers. The elaborateness of their presentation has grown considerably over the last few years but there are three principal elements. These are the **Profit and Loss account**; the **Balance Sheet** and the **Sources and Uses of Funds Statement** (which is called the **Consolidated Cash Flow Statement** in listed companies' accounts). These accounts must distinguish between **parent** and **group** (consolidated) figures where this is appropriate. This is explained in Chapter 11.

Highly important but not very illuminating is the **Auditors' Report**. This shows whether the accounts of the company being reported on were compiled according to recognised accounting standards and whether they give a 'true and fair view' of the period being reported. If they do not, then the auditor is required to 'qualify' his approval of the accounts in some way. Some qualifications – especially in private companies – may be trivial; others may be less so. *Any* qualification of a listed company's accounts can be regarded as a warning sign to investors.

Notes to the Financial Statements

After these sections come the **Notes to the Accounts**. These are separated from the numerical component of the accounts but are still very much part of them. Boring and complicated as these may look, they often hold the keys to a full understanding of what is going on in the accounts of the company and will usually extend to several pages. They are numbered to coincide with small numbers you will find inserted adjacent to the main numbers in the body of the accounts, so that they can be easily cross-referenced by the reader.

These Notes are extremely valuable to the analyst because they explain much of the detail that has to be left out of the main accounts because of the demands of simple presentation. Although they might look tedious they should not be neglected. Careful study of the Notes will show how the business is developing and will make clear those points that would otherwise be difficult to understand.

The range and scope of the Notes is so wide that it is difficult to give an example that shows exactly how helpful they can be. But take Fixed Assets as an example: the Notes to the Accounts for fixed assets will show exactly how the charge for depreciation for the year is made up and will allow the analyst to have a good stab at assessing what it might be for the coming year.

In addition, they will show the composition of the fixed asset register (the list of all the assets that the business possesses) so that a fair assessment can be made of the likely capital expenditure for the coming year. (The fixed asset/ depreciation Notes will show the retirements from the register and the volume of additions, reinforcing the guesses that can be made about forthcoming expenditure.)

How do we make sense of all this overwhelming volume of information?

Chapter 5:

Thinking Like an Analyst Part 2

The natural breaks
First impressions of the accounts
Holding information in your head
Spotting trends
Preliminary conclusion – with some guide questions

I have already said that you must begin to think like an analyst when you pick up a set of accounts. You must establish a critical attitude to the information that you are going to use. At first sight a set of accounts may appear a bit daunting and more than a bit complicated. But what you must bear in mind – as with all tasks that involve figure work – is that there are a number of 'natural breaks' in the numbers that mean that things can be taken in small chunks that are more easily worked with than a huge spread of numbers.

The order of break is largely up to you but obviously the three main ones are the three main sections of the accounts: the Profit and Loss as a unit; then the Balance Sheet as a unit; and finally the Sources and Uses of Funds as a unit.

Within each of these there will be further breaks that you can look at – and, as we shall learn later, there will be the same breaks for building up a prediction of a company's performance as there are for deconstructing the accounts.

With this three-part division in mind, there are three other steps to getting to grips with the accounts:

First,

fix the shape of the accounts in your mind. This is a bit like making sure that you have the map the right way up before you navigate your way along an unfamiliar road. It involves nothing very complicated and merely means becoming familiar with the layout of the accounts so that you know what information is available and where it is.

Second,

pick out significant elements that you think might be of value to investigate further. If something looks very complicated or particularly interesting – maybe a complicated Note to the accounts or a long description of a particular project that the business is involved with – then mark it as being a valuable further source of information.

And third,

look at the overall performance of the company. Just cast your mind over the comparative information that the accounts set out. Year end or Statutory Accounts will show you the position at the end of both the year being reported on and the previous year, so you can very easily make some rapid comparative assessments of how well or badly the business did by simply looking at the two sets of figures which are set out side by side.

Putting this into Practice

While the accounts may be dull, grey and boringly presented – because few people are actively interested in them and so why waste effort in appealing to these sad characters anyway? – they usually come wrapped up in a glossy report that forms the first-named half (and superior half as far as most people are concerned) of the report and accounts.

In this the directors have a statutory obligation to report on the company's experiences during the year and, in large companies at least, usually take the opportunity to put the best face of the company to the light.

The report of the directors to the members of a company is the medium by which the company can preen itself a bit. Interesting and useful information can often be found on projects, products and developments in the company's services. This is often accompanied by revealing information about the market place or statistical information that cannot be displayed satisfactorily in the numerical part of the accounts.

Such information also gives clues to some of the darker prospects for the company – maybe details of problems with overseas contracts for civil engineers; problems with suppliers or customers for manufacturing businesses; land shortages for housebuilders; or product shortages for food processors or supermarkets. Sometimes you will see mention of the phrase 'on a like-for-like basis'. This means quite simply that the analysis has been adjusted so that the structure of the business this year is being compared with the way it was last year. For instance, a supermarket chain which has acquired another chain of shops might give a like-for-like comparison that is based on the same number of square metres of floor space as it had before the acquisition so that the 'organic' (that is, without the effects of any acquisition) growth of sales can be demonstrated.

This information can be very useful for the outside analyst who otherwise has no direct access to the company, since it gives insights into areas that are usually only available to professional analysts. They make it their business to know the detail of a company's activities but some of the raw material that they use is, of course, the report of the directors!

Look too at the details of the personnel referred to in the accounts – the directors must be identified and senior managers are often shown as well. Do changes in the ranks of these people mean that something has gone wrong? Businesses with a public face are often not very tolerant of failure among their senior managers because of the impact of failure in a project on share prices. The departure of a senior manager between the issue of two sets of accounts can often be an indication that things are not as they should be in one particular area of the business.

I cannot go into every detail of information that can be gleaned from a critical review of the report and accounts because what might be learnt is simply too big to be categorised. Anything and everything might turn up. Pictures, words or tables might throw light on some detail in the accounts that would otherwise rest in obscurity. What is required of the investigator is the ability to hold detail in the mind ready for matching up with a small detail in another part of the document to make something out of the combination.

First Impressions are Usually Right

Regardless of whether the accounts come from a listed company or a private company, when you are fixing the shape of the accounts in your mind (rather then the actual numbers themselves) **think about these things first:**

Is there lots of detail?

Is the chairman's report very extensive or have the directors chosen to say very little about trading and future prospects?

If the company is not listed and is of a certain size it has the option of filing 'abbreviated accounts'. Has the company chosen to take advantage of these small company provisions which mean that it need not produce full accounts? (If so the amount of information that you can usefully harvest will be very limited.)

Are the Notes to the Accounts very detailed (which may well mean that the company has a complicated financial history)?

Are there many different categories of shares? That may suggest something to you about the way that the company has been financed.

As you leaf through the accounts try to hold as much of any possible inter-relationships in your mind as possible. One of the tricks that a good analyst will be able to perform is to remember a small detail and relate that to another piece of information to which it is perhaps not obviously linked to produce a further piece of information that will be of value to him. You have to think laterally as well as in straight lines.

Once you have had this cursory look, read the chairman's statement carefully and read the captions to the photographs and illustrations (if there are any). Most quoted companies spend a good deal of time and money on getting their reports as well-presented as possible since they recognise that these documents have the power to impress shareholders if they look good and tell a good story. As they have spent all this effort to try to tell you something, use the report to wring as much out of it as you can.

As you read, pick out features that you think might be of interest when you come to study the accounts properly. If there are divisional results or details of major contracts, for instance, then flag these by either marking them up with a highlighter or a piece of sticky notepad. Or make notes to help you as you go along.

Turning now to the **overall performance**, always look first at last year's numbers shown alongside in the accounts and familiarise yourself with the performance of the company in the year prior to the one that has just been reported upon, so that you have established a benchmark in your own mind against which to measure the year in which you are really interested. Then compare last year with this year.

This comparison doesn't have to be very sophisticated – just look at the way the numbers move – or the way that they 'trend' as the professional analysts might say. See if there is a consistent movement up or down or if there has been a sudden blip in one direction or another. If there is a persistent trend then you may be able to tell if this is likely to continue ... or maybe something in the written reports of the directors or chairman will tell you that the run has come to an end.

Finally look again at both years together, this time for pointers from sections in the accounts:

Was the performance of the business better or worse than last year? (Look in the P&L or the financial highlights, or read the report of the chairman.)

Does it appear that cash was used up? (You can find this out by comparing the figures for this year and last year under the heading for Bank Balances – which might be shown as 'cash at bank or in hand' in the Balance Sheet.)

Did borrowing increase? (Look at the appropriate section in the Balance Sheet again. This time it will be shown under the Current Liabilities *and* the Creditors' sections, and identified as borrowings. You will find an example in Appendix 2.)

Was turnover up or down? (Look at the top item of the Profit and Loss account and compare this year's figure with last year's.) However, don't treat this too literally – strangely a company can sometimes produce more profit on less turnover.

If the company is listed, how was the performance per share in comparison with last year in terms of the dividend that was paid out? (You'll probably find this information at the bottom of the Profit and Loss account or in the financial highlights. Just compare the figures again to give you a rough idea.)

When you've done this you can make a preliminary conclusion about the year – just summarising what you have found if nothing more suggests itself to you – and write it down. You can come back to this later on in your examination of the accounts. Some of the things that you have written down will be right; some may need modification. Be prepared to change your impressions in the light of better understanding of the detail. Regardless of whether you change anything or not, the act of writing these things down will help you to organise your thoughts both now and later on.

Chapter 6:

Some Basic Concepts

What a 'full set of accounts' is
The basic structure of a set of accounts
Definitions of the three individual parts
The most important distinctions in looking at accounts:
  – TIME
  – CASH versus PROFIT

'The Full Set of Accounts'

A full set of accounts is composed of three elements:

1)   A Profit and Loss account
2)   A Balance Sheet
3)   A Sources and Uses (or Sources and Applications) of
     Funds Statement.

All of these have to be present in order to have a full
appreciation of what the numbers can tell you – even for
only one accounting period. Only when all three are in place
can you hope to make some reasonable guesses about the
trends that may underlie the raw presentation. With only
two of the three, the amount of information that can be
drawn out is extremely limited. The availability of only one
element of those listed will make the job of producing a
sensible interpretation of trends virtually impossible.

Each of the three components is dealt with at length in
separate chapters but for now I will simply define each one
so that you know what they all do.

Definition 1:

The **Profit and Loss account** of a business summarises the income and expenses of a company over a stated *period* of time to show whether it made a profit (income exceeded costs) or a loss (costs exceeded income).

Definition 2:

The **Balance Sheet** of a business shows its value at a stated *point* in time. It does this by identifying the individual components of its worth which are either assets (things owned by the business) or liabilities (things that the business owes to others) displayed against each other to give a 'net' value. This amount is then shown to 'balance' the amount, separately calculated, which represents the combined shareholders' (owners') interests in the business.

The values shown are *cumulative for all the time that the company has been in existence* until the date when the Balance Sheet was made up. So the Balance Sheet includes all the profits that were made (after taxes and dividends have been paid), or all the deficits that arose when the company made losses, since it came into existence.

Definition 3:

The **Sources and Uses of Funds Statement** of a business (or, in the case of a PLC, the **Consolidated Cash Flow Statement**) shows where the cash used by a business came from and where it went, over a stated *period* of time.

What the Accounts Really Are

It is important to realise that the accounts that are presented for each accounting period are the sum of:

1) (Probably) a very large number of individual transactions added together; and that

2) In the case of Statutory Accounts, they have been recorded over a period of perhaps a year, perhaps as much as fifteen months; and

3) That they consist of a mix between cash items (where cash has actually moved from one party to another) and profit items that may be the result of only book movements of numbers that may *or may not* have been backed up by real movements in cash or in other resources.

The Most Important Distinctions

The detail of all the features listed above will be explained as we go along but for now the most important things to grasp about accounts are that:

1) They contain information about *time*; and

2) *Cash* and *profit* are **not** the same thing.

You should also note that the Balance Sheet shows *information correct for one point in time only* (in fact for one specific date only) while the Profit and Loss account and the Statement of Sources and Uses of Funds both show *changes over a stated period of time*.

The point about accounts relating to a period of time is easy to understand with a little thought (although it becomes more complicated at anything beyond a superficial level, as you will see later). However, there is another point about time which it is also important to grasp from the outset. Published accounts usually refer to a period of time that may be long gone: UK registered companies whose shares are not listed on a Stock Exchange are allowed eleven months' grace in getting their accounts to the Registrar of Companies (which is when they become publicly available).

This means that when you are using published, Statutory Accounts, the information on which you are basing your work can be the better part of two years old.

A great deal of water will have flowed under the bridge in that time. Think about how different the components of your financial circumstances probably were two years ago!

However, the most significant feature of accounts, apart from the time problem, that some people find hard to comprehend, is the distinction between *cash* and *profit*.

The essential point to grasp is that the profit that a business makes is *not* the cash that ends up in the business; it is just the number that completes the Profit and Loss account. It *may* be the same as the amount of cash that the business generates but if so this would be a coincidence of numbers.

The final number in a Profit and Loss account (before tax is levied) is really an indication of the amount on which there will be obligation to pay taxes. The profit after tax figure is really only a technical figure that is almost valueless for analytical purposes, aside from providing some basis for judging whether the business can afford to pay a dividend of some sort to its owners.

It is broadly true that profit will (usually) turn into cash – however, it may not do so and it would be perilous to rely on it doing so. It is possible to make apparently respectable profits and yet consume cash dramatically and bankrupt a business. Paradoxically, businesses recording losses in their Profit and Loss accounts may still produce cash and sustain an apparently wobbly existence for some time. You will see the detail of how all this works later.

The ability to distinguish between cash and profit is what marks out someone who properly understands a report and accounts – and who probably has a reasonable chance of running a business successfully.

Section Two

Chapter 7:

Introduction to the P&L

What the P&L does
The Clock analogy
Different kinds of profit
Why break down profit?

The P&L account is the major tool at the disposal of the analyst. The P&L allows him or her to peer into a business and see how that business works. It's not a bad idea to think of it as showing movement. Investigating the P&L is a bit like looking at the movement of a mechanical clock with the back off: you can see all the tiny pieces of the mechanism that contribute to changing the winding of the spring into a movement of the hands.

In contrast, but to use the same analogy, observing the Balance Sheet is more like looking at the face of the clock – it shows a particular position at a particular moment in time. By comparison with the P&L, the Balance Sheet does not readily reveal many of the secrets of how a business is developing. However, it is supportive to the P&L for most of the purposes of interpretation and analysis.

In this respect it is a little bit like the Sources and Uses of Funds Statement. However, since the S&U also acts as the link between the Balance Sheet and the P&L in the accounts – a bit like the movement mechanism that transfers the energy of the spring to turn the hands on the clock face –

the latter can be regarded in some ways as the more useful of the two.

For these reasons most of the analysis that needs to be done in forecasting is done by reference to the P&L. There is a worked example of how to get quite elaborate information from a simple P&L at Appendix 1. You should look at that now to get an idea of what can be done, even though I shall not discuss some of the terms that are used in the illustration until later. If you are going to use it properly, you need to understand just what it is that the P&L can do. The information provided by the P&L account shows:

1)   How much profit a business made overall; and
2)   How much was made at a variety of levels or points in the business.

There are three levels in which analysts are interested – 'gross profitability', 'operating profit' and 'pre-tax profit' (all of which are defined below, although not all of them will be applicable to every business).

Definition 4:

At its simplest, **Gross Profit** is the overall profit that a business makes from its income, after deducting **only** the costs of raw materials and that expenditure incurred directly in the process of turning them into finished products for sale – and *before* deducting all other running costs.

By convention, the cost of raw materials and direct labour is known as the '**Cost of Sales**' – although this term has no legal definition for use in Statutory Accounts. The **Gross Margin** is the same amount as the Gross Profit but expressed as a percentage of the turnover rather than as a number. Service businesses, incidentally, do not generally have a Gross Profit or

Gross Margin since they have no raw materials to buy in.

Definition 5:

Operating profit is the profit that a business makes after deducting from the gross profit all of its other costs *with the exception of finance charges*. (Service businesses start their profit calculations with operating profits.) This may sometimes be called the 'net profit', although this term is more usually applied to the profit on an individual item sold. The **Net Margin** is the same number but expressed as a percentage of turnover.

Definition 6:

Pretax Profits are the profits left from taking all the costs that a business incurs – raw materials costs, employment costs, premises costs, and all the other costs, including finance costs – from its income.

The Purposes of Breaking Down Profitability

These definitions are fairly straightforward and it should be relatively easy to see how they must apply to a small and simple business.

The purposes of breaking profit down into these three levels are:

1) To enable management to control the business more effectively by identifying exactly which parts of the business absorb most of the income that sales generate
2) To enable management and outside shareholders to see how efficiently the business is being operated – by comparing the profit achieved at any given level in the business with that achieved by competitors at similar points.

If truth is told, then all that the P&L shows for most businesses is the *average* level of profit made by that business on all its activities over the period of time for which the P&L is being calculated. This is true for any business.

However, once a business moves beyond one product and one worker or begins to stockpile raw materials and finished goods, the process of accounting becomes much more complicated – and consequently the picture presented by the P&L becomes more blurry.

You might think that it would be possible to get round the problem of complication and distortion by producing lots of mini sets of accounts. Perhaps businesses could produce more detailed Profit and Loss accounts for individual product lines, for instance.

Unfortunately this will not work. Apart from the complexity of doing all that accounting work, if a business has several different products, then, unless it can reduce them all to single product businesses each with their own premises, their own systems, employees and administration, these mini-accounts would all be subject to a whole variety of estimates, apportionments and omissions. If there is any form of common usage of raw materials or labour or premises with another product, then errors and distortions are bound to arise.

Inevitably, therefore, the practical benefits of producing more and more things, using the same production resources, will conflict with the ability to keep records simple.

So it is important to realise from the outset, as I said above, that in all but very simple businesses (say, one man, one product, probably no manufacturing), the P&L is an *average* of what happened over the time for all the activities that were undertaken.

Despite all the verbiage and accounting boilerplate that surrounds the presentation of accounts, to expect anything else is expecting an unreasonable level of accuracy. To claim that the Profit and Loss account shows exactly what happened to a business during a year is falling into a deep analytical trap. The Profit and Loss account *by itself* will show very little about a business that can be used to make a sensible and balanced evaluation of how well or how badly a business is doing.

Chapter 8:

The P&L Account: More Terms and Definitions

---

*The components of the P&L
*Points to watch out for in dealing with each

Now that we have looked at the basics of the Profit and Loss account it is appropriate to define in detail some of the terms that will be encountered.

Some American companies use the term 'income statement' in describing what is called a P&L elsewhere. There is also the confusion that can arise when people talk about an 'income and expenditure' statement. This is *not* the same thing as a P&L, although it forms the basis for the P&L – with some adjustments.

Obviously, unless we are all talking about the same thing and using the same terms there is going to be confusion. So let's get our terms straight and understand what it is that we are talking about.

Turnover/Sales

All P&L accounts start with **sales revenue** – the amount of income that actually came into the business during the period under consideration.

Points to watch out for in dealing with Turnover

1) Definitions

The definition of turnover may vary depending on the type of business at which you are looking. This point is impor-

41

tant when you are considering two businesses side-by-side or two sets of accounts from the same company, or when you are looking at Statutory, as opposed to Management, Accounts. You also have to check the definition used by the auditors when they approved the final accounts for the company to make sure that it is the same between two sets of accounts. You can find these definitions in the Notes to the Accounts.

To give an example of this, a manufacturing business will typically state its turnover as being the revenue that it generated from the sale of its products during the year. For the purpose of Statutory Accounts (as opposed to Management accounts) it *must* show that revenue net of (after taking off) any discounts that it offered its customers for prompt payment of their accounts.

2)   *Accounts Formats*

However, if you are looking at Management accounts, you may find instead that those same discounts have been added back as part of the **Cost of Sales**. They are sometimes taken together with the transport costs that the business had to bear (both inward and outward carriage, since these are both costs to the business) and then **netted off** against discounts that have been received from the company's own suppliers for prompt settlement. (This term means setting two amounts off against each other to produce a 'net' amount that has to be applied positively or negatively to the accounts.) So bear in mind which style of accounting is being adopted.

3)   *Different Types of Business*

Turnover for a manufacturing company is reasonably straightforward. However, if the company is in, say, advertising, it may include as part of its turnover the cost of the advertising space in newspapers/magazines, or on posters or radio or television that it bought for its clients. This will swell the recorded turnover dramatically. Other service businesses or professional practices may likewise include in turnover the cost of bought-in goods which are then recharged to clients' accounts, usually with some form of administration or handling charge being stuck on to the bills as they go past.

4)   Inclusions in the Accounts

Almost all businesses show their turnover net of Value Added Tax (Statutory Accounts *must* do so) since this is an in-and-out consideration and not part of the business's own income. Some very simple businesses might not choose to do so, perhaps because of preference (or perhaps because of ignorance!) or because they are not large enough to reach the required threshold for VAT registration (which is the point where they are able to reclaim the cost of their VAT-ed supplies back from the Customs and Excise).

To make this point about not including VAT clear, think about what the company was doing. It wasn't getting the money for itself in adding the tax to all that it took from its customers, it was acting as tax collector for the Government. (However, you can make a mental note that the cash position of a company may benefit from the interest received from the deposit of money for the VAT that the company has collected and is holding for the Customs and Excise until such time as payment is due each quarter.)

Incidentally, you may sometimes hear the verbal shorthand term 'top line' when people are referring to accounts – as in, 'That will affect the top line'. The top line is the turnover line and is abbreviated to 'top line' because, quite simply, it is the top line of the P&L account.

Cost of Sales

After turnover comes the **Cost of Sales** line. This is again open to problems of definition since it can also be the rag-bag line where discounts are recorded and possibly 'netted off'. Some *Management accounts* will show discounts to the business and discounts offered by the company netted off at this stage. As has already been mentioned there is no strict legal/accounting definition for Cost of Sales for use in Statutory Accounts.

Points to watch out for in dealing with Cost of Sales

The **Cost of Sales** line is calculated by taking the Balance Sheet value of stock in hand at the end of the year, *less* the Balance Sheet value of the stock that was carried at the start of the year *plus* the cost of any purchases made in between those times. (It is also normal to allow for discounts for early payment or bulk orders, given or received, and charges for carriage in both directions, inward and outward.)

To this are added the costs of direct labour *only* employed in turning raw materials into saleable product. These costs (raw materials and direct labour) are sometimes referred to as **Prime Costs**.

You can see that this might begin to get complicated in definitional terms! The complications that will arise from Current Cost Accounting, if it is applied (see Appendix 4), can make the calculation even more tricky.

Alternative Formats

There is another format (offered by the Companies' Act 1985) which requires companies to reveal the changes in their stocks of finished goods and part-finished goods and then to set out the amounts of raw materials that they have purchased, displaying wages and salaries separately and making no distinction between direct and indirect labour (that is, labour not employed directly in turning raw materials into product). This format is very rarely used in Management accounts but is optional for Statutory Accounts. Given that it makes no distinction between direct and indirect labour, it is theoretically more suited to service businesses; however, it is quite unusual.

If this variation format is chosen, then it has follow-on effects in forcing the business into displaying all staff costs broken out into direct costs of employment – wages and salaries – and then into indirect costs too – social security costs and pension costs.

Distribution and Administrative Costs

These chunks of money are, quite simply, what they say – all the other costs associated with running any business. Statutory Accounts will take transport costs into account at this point whereas Management accounts may have made allowance for them earlier on as we have seen. (Management accounts do this to ensure that managers see the extent to which the costs of carriage affect profit.)

These categories of expenditure bring into the calculations the costs of all the other staff (meaning *other* than those only engaged directly in turning raw materials into saleable goods) employed in the business, together with all their associated costs, and the general costs of running the company – insurance, phones, postage, stationery, rents, computers, heat, light and power, and so on.

Incidentally, the costs of fines or penalties incurred during business operations cannot legally be taken into account in calculating the taxable profits.

Finally, in the list of deductions made to the P&L we come to **depreciation**. Depreciation is charged at this point – after all the ascertainable 'real' costs have been charged. And, because it is quite a complicated subject, depreciation is worth a brief chapter to itself!

Chapter 9:

Depreciation

The subject of depreciation causes so much trouble in understanding accounts that it is worth giving some extra space to it so that some of the common pitfalls can be avoided.

One of the first problems in analysing the depreciation number carried in accounts is knowing where to find it. Although it affects the P&L profoundly, you will not usually find it on the face of the P&L account. The amount of depreciation charged against the P&L will be found – in Statutory Accounts, at least – in the Notes to the Financial Statements, where it is listed as one of the components affecting operating profit. It will also, of course, show up in the Balance Sheet.

There is often much confusion among managers about depreciation. And this confusion is not limited to managers. I would guess that, if you asked an accountant, a banker and an engineer all employed in business what depreciation is, you would probably get three different answers.

What Depreciation Does and What it Does NOT Do

The Classic Definition:

The purpose of depreciation is to provide for the financial effects of machinery or other equipment

46

wearing out, that are brought about by usage in production of a good or service.

The purpose of depreciation is **NOT** to:

1)   Provide a sinking fund for the replacement of goods as
      they get worn out
2)   Indicate how fast a piece of machinery reaches the end
      of its useful life
3)   Allow for inflation in calculating how much a replace-
      ment piece of machinery will cost

or

4)   Provide a way of working out what the HP payments
      should be on a piece of machinery.

All of which I have seen or heard managers describe as the
purpose of depreciation.

To make clear what depreciation really is, let's suppose a
piece of machinery costs £1,000 and is expected to last 5
years before it is worn out. During that time it will produce
1,000 items of the particular good it can make every year.
The purpose of depreciation is to load the accounts, during
each of these years, with an appropriate cost brought about
by the wear and tear that the production of each of the
individual goods will bring about. In accounting for this
effect in the P&L, this factor is applied to the annual
general administrative expenses, so as properly to reflect
the true cost that the production of each good made in any
one year, ought to absorb from the cost of the machine. One
way of looking at it is to think of depreciation as establish-
ing more accurately the real cost-price for the goods being
produced.

To return to our example, each good produced should
therefore bear one five thousandth of the cost of the
machine if its real economic cost of production is to be
calculated and a sensible cost-price is to be established for

each product. You could, of course, say that the first good manufactured bears the entire cost of the machine and every other piece comes free of capital costs but you wouldn't find many takers for the first one off the run! You might find lots of buyers for the remaining 4,999 pieces if their individual price included nothing for depreciation but you would remain stuck with a loss of almost £1,000 on that first one that didn't sell . . .

In this *economic sense* depreciation is not the afterthought that it sometimes appears to be when looking at accounts, but is a prime determinant of the costs of a good.

So, in every set of accounts, you find that the accountants remove from the profits a value which they have calculated for depreciation. They do it on the P&L by *adding* the depreciation figure into the 'operating' costs – the **general administrative expenses** – before that total is deducted from the Gross Profit. On the Balance Sheet, as you will see in Chapter 12, it comes off the figure for tangible Fixed Assets.

In arriving at selling prices for goods, managers have to make an upward allowance for the cost of machinery per item produced. That is why the cost of depreciation, which you can think of as wear and tear, has to be removed from the Profit and Loss account. To leave it in would effectively be forgetting to count the cost.

From this it follows that the amount set aside for depreciation is NOT a monetary, spendable amount like money stashed under the bed for a rainy day. It is not hard cash removed from the business. Neither is it a sum which the business sets aside for replacement. It's more like your personal tax allowance but applied in this case to a company rather than an individual.

The amount of depreciation charged in any set of accounts is calculated on an agreed theoretical basis which varies from business to business but is always to be found written down in the 'Notes to the Financial Statements' which follow the numbers' pages.

Chapter 10:

The Balance Sheet: Structure and Purpose

*Introducing the Balance Sheet
*Various formats
*The three characteristics:
  – prudence
  – control
  – completeness

Hopefully, readers will be familiar with the basic concept of a Balance Sheet in the sense that it displays and 'balances' the shareholders' investment in and ownership of a company, against the assets of the business as they stand on the day chosen for the end of an accounting period.

You might like to look again at **Definition 2** given in Chapter 6 to refresh your memory about what a Balance Sheet represents.

In essence, the Balance Sheet takes the starting position of the company from the time that it was created – at the time that shareholders' funds were first subscribed – and then adds to that all the retained profits ploughed back in, or losses, that occur subsequently. Losses, of course, diminish the value of the company by taking value away from shareholders' funds. Any additions to the assets that are made out of cash increases brought about by trading, the introduction of further funds from shareholders and the injection of loans from outside parties, such as banks or finance houses, are also reflected in the value of the Balance

Sheet. Against all these it sets the debts that the business owes other people.

The presentation of the Balance Sheet has changed over the years according to fashion among accountants and it is most usually seen nowadays as a list of items going down the page rather than spread across the page in a 'lefthand-righthand' format. Appendix 2 shows a typical Balance Sheet for an imaginary company.

In England and Wales, the structure of the Balance Sheet for Statutory Accounts is governed by law (the Companies' Acts 1986 and later) and the Stock Exchange imposes additional rules for the format of accounts presented by listed companies. Strictly speaking, again, a private company can choose to do whatever it likes in the preparation of its own Management accounts, subject to the legal requirement to keep proper books, but most will follow the standard format dictated by the Statements of Standard Accounting Practice (the 'SSAPs') which are published by the regulating bodies of the accounting profession and are internationally recognised.

It used to be the case under the old style of displaying a Balance Sheet that there would be assets on one side and liabilities on the other. This has now changed dramatically so that what is now shown are the funds subscribed (and generated from sales) on one side and the use to which they have been put on the other. This means that assets and liabilities now share the same 'half' of the Balance Sheet. While this may be confusing to the beginner, it is a much neater distinction from the theoretical point of view – although less easy to describe!

One overhang of the old format, though, is that most people still talk about 'sides' of a Balance Sheet. This convention still makes it much easier to describe what is going on than referring to cumbersome headings.

In truth, the niceties of the format of the Balance Sheet are not particularly important since the fundamental point is that one half of the Balance Sheet must be balanced in value by the other half. Up and down or side to side, it doesn't really matter; what is crucial is that the business's assets (the Net Assets employed – being total assets less *all* liabilities) have to match the shareholders' interests (the amounts that were subscribed by the shareholders plus any retained profits that have subsequently accrued to them). All the Balance Sheet is really doing is showing where the money that shareholders have committed to the business has been applied in running the business.

Balance Sheets have (at least) three important characteristics – two of which we shall deal with now and one of which will be dealt with slightly later in the chapter. The first of these is that they must be compiled *prudently*: the values which are contained in the Balance Sheet for individual entries have to be placed in there only after the managers and auditors have assured themselves that they reflect the true valuation of the item – the lowest value that an asset would actually realise if the business were forced to sell it; or the highest value of a debt if it were to be called. In this respect it is also important to appreciate the sequence of calculation: the Profit and Loss account can only be calculated after the Balance Sheet values have been determined – which means, effectively, after stock has been counted and any adjustments to its value as a consequence of spoilage or other assessment of sale-ability have been made.

The second characteristic – also as a consequence of the order of calculation – is that the values in the Balance Sheet are the *controlling* values, which are transferred into the P&L and the S&U and referred to when appropriate – for instance in using stock values to determine the Cost of Sales.

Most text books describe what a Balance Sheet is by describing its components rather than its purpose. A description of the bits of a Balance Sheet follows in the next chapter so that, for instance, you become familiar with some of the more arcane types of share capital that you might come across in smaller company Balance Sheets.

But for now we need to describe what a Balance Sheet *does*. Everyone is familiar with the basic concept of a Balance

Sheet in their own lives. You know by looking at your own cash position – what you have and what you owe – that you can only spend up to the limit of your available cash resources and remaining credit. And you use your own personal 'Balance Sheet' in terms of cash books and bank statements to work out how much cash you have accumulated during the year.

The company or business Balance Sheet takes this a stage further by showing the position since the company was born – it is very unlikely that you have a complete record of your annual financial transactions since you were born! – and it goes further than that by giving clues to every major financial event in the life of the business. Careful scrutiny of a Balance Sheet and comparison with previous ones will tell you a great deal about the ups and downs of a business's trading and the way that it managed to raise or dispose of cash. It also shows scars if you know how to look for them!

So we have arrived at another characteristic of a Balance Sheet – and perhaps its most important. It is *complete* – it leaves nothing out; everything is accounted for. And, since every Balance Sheet starts where the last one ended, and the previous one by definition must be complete, the entire record of a business's financial history is encapsulated within its most recent Balance Sheet.

Because of this completeness, what a Balance Sheet can also do – if you read it carefully – is to give you a clue as to the financial future of a business.

This is because the Balance Sheet has to account for all the financial obligations that it can be foreseen a business will have to meet. So, for instance, when you look at the liabilities half of the Balance Sheet, you can make an assessment of creditors' payments that will have to be met in the short term; what dividends are going to be paid out; and when any large repayments of debt are due.

You may come across the terms 'strong' and 'weak' when Balance Sheets are being discussed. These are relative rather than absolute terms and refer – usually – to the amount of debt in the Balance Sheet and the amounts of shareholders' funds in proportion to the business's cash requirements. The related concept of gearing we shall discuss in Chapter 20.

Looking at the assets side of the Balance Sheet as we shall see later, you can, with a little comparison of turnover and the appropriate levels of stock, and of the debtors and creditors from last year's information, get a feel for whether stock will need to be increased to meet current levels of activity (or whether it is swollen and will have to be run down), for how fast debtor payments can be collected, and for whether the business's cash balances are sufficient for its current level of trading activity.

Going on from there you can go back to look at the totality of the Balance Sheet and make an assessment of whether shareholders might have to stump up some more cash to keep the business going or expand it.

We shall look at the mechanics of some of these tricks of the trade later but for the moment it is probably enough to indicate *how* these things can be done. For instance, it is possible to gather an idea of whether a company will require cash for working capital (see page 68) by comparing the rate at which stock is turned over with the length of time that creditors have to wait for their money and debtors pay the company what they owe (see page 122). If there is a disparity between all these then there may be a need for extra cash. So, when you come to produce a cash flow forecast or, more likely, a predicted Sources and Uses of Funds Statement for the business, you will be able to use the Balance Sheet information to help you ascertain the rate of cash accumulation or cash consumption.

All this comes with practice and with growing familiarity with the look of a Balance Sheet. But first let's see what the individual terms on a Balance Sheet mean.

Chapter 11:

The Balance Sheet: Terms and Definitions – Capital Side

*The difference between Parent and Group accounts
*Share capital and the types of share capital
*Reserves

Just as we defined terms for the P&L account in order to avoid confusion, so we will have a look at the Balance Sheet and do the same for that.

Companies which are the parent companies of groups are required to show **parent company accounts** and the **group accounts** separately and you may well find that there are two sets of headings – group and company – which identify the respective entities. This is the same, of course, for the P&L.

Usually, and for most practical purposes, the 'parent company' accounts can be ignored since they are of no real significance. However, occasionally, you will find quirks of share structure or of dividend policy, or of associate company ownership that may be best understood by reference to the company accounts rather than to the group.

Subtracting the company Balance Sheet figures from the group figures may – but not very often it has to be said – display interesting nuggets of information about quirks of corporate governance. Why is there a fixed asset of disproportionate value in the assets of the parent? Could that be the London flat used by the chief executive or the aeroplanes used for company business? Or is there a simpler explanation?

As we have already seen, the two sides of the Balance Sheet used to be called the assets side and the liabilities side but this distinction is now redundant following the change in format to up-and-down rather than left-and-right. Balance Sheets often now appear without any specific headings except for perhaps 'Capital' and 'Represented By'.

The first thing that a Balance Sheet shows on the share capital side – chronologically, if not always in display terms – is, not surprisingly, the amount of **share capital** that has been subscribed to start the business.

Definition 7:

> **Share capital** is the money subscribed by the owners of a company in order to allow it to trade. Once in place it cannot be reduced without a special process approved by the High Court. If there is a reduction of one class of shares then this can only be done out of the proceeds of an issue of a fresh class of shares or out of distributable profits. Consequently, the principal feature of share capital is that it is permanently in place.

Share capital, which is also known as '**equity**', can be in a variety of forms. The most common is **Ordinary shares**. These can be sub-divided into a variety of further classes, possibly with different voting rights, so you can have A Ordinaries or B Ordinaries, for instance:

Preferred Ordinary (in which the shares might get prior rights to any dividends);

Participating Preferred Ordinary (in which the shares will have some variable rights to a portion of the pretax profits before dividends are declared);

Convertible shares (which will be able to convert into a different class of shares, probably with more valuable share rights, at some time);

Cumulative shares (which never lose the right to a dividend even if it is 'passed' – that is, not paid – in any year so that arrears of dividends on these shares have to be paid off before any other dividend can be paid);

Or even **Cumulative Convertible Participating Preferred Ordinary** (CCPPOs) – and you can work that one out for yourself!

The wilder reaches of share capital classes are generally not found outside the ranks of companies which are funded with venture capital. This is because there are certain strictures imposed by the rules of the Stock Exchange on what types of shares a company can have when it is admitted to the Official Lists.

Whatever their names, all the shares described above have the same characteristic – the initial value that they represent cannot be removed from the business. In England and Wales, if a company is formed with an initial share capital of £100 then that £100 will stay with it for its life or it will be added to. It cannot be reduced except by permission of the High Court. So, if the company's regulations do allow certain types of shares to be redeemed, then an equivalent value of a different sort (perhaps a share that the company already has) has to be created. See also the paragraphs on Revaluation Reserves, page 60, for a further examination of how this is done.

Loan Capital

Although it will not appear in the same part of the Balance Sheet – since it is not share capital or equity but a form of borrowing – we can usefully deal with another form of capital here.

Capital can also be subscribed in the form of **loans**. Sometimes these may also have rights to convert into an appointed number of shares at some time in the future, in which case they would be known, not surprisingly, as **Convertible Loan Stock** (sometimes called CLS). However, since loan stock can be repaid just like any other loan, it is not a permanent part of the business's capital base.

CLS and **Redeemable Loan Stock** (RLS) are often issued by companies raising money from investment funds. Since they are loans they will appear on the liabilities section of the Balance Sheet (which we deal with in the next chapter) rather than with the equity. For a small company, redeemable loan stock and convertible loan stock are probably brought into being at the same time as some of the shares. In fact, they are often the signature of a venture capital investment since the loans can have security attached to them which will protect part of the total investment in the event of some trading catastrophe. This has the beneficial effect for the investor of minimising the amount of money that is totally at risk. (It is possible also to have Convertible Redeemable Loan Stocks that may convert into equity if they are not repaid in a certain period of time. This is a certain clue to a venture capital investment and is seldom found except in private companies.)

In addition the fact that, in the case of RLS, the money is redeemable, will enable the investors to get part of their original investment out before the realisation of the equity portion. This can enhance the value of their investment, since they will still retain their share of the ownership of the business through their equity holdings even though the loans are repaid.

In the case of CLS they may get the chance to buy some more of the equity of the company for a previously-set price if certain targets are not achieved, often using what is called a 'ratchet' mechanism. There are also other technical reasons why Convertibles are often issued which are concerned with the valuation of the investment at the time that the investors make their investment; these are slightly too complex for us to go into here.

The presence of a Redeemable Loan Stock carries the

assumption that the company will raise enough money at some point in the future (either by borrowing again or by issuing shares) to buy the loan stock back. This point is often defined, so that the loan stock is classified, for instance, as Redeemable Loan Stock 2020/2025. The dates at the end of the classification indicate over what period the company intends to redeem the loan. Where the loan stock has no redemption period indicated then it must be assumed that it is perpetual loan stock. But, confusingly, this is still not permanent capital.

This loan stock can be sold to investors who might want to find a guaranteed rate of interest. If they in turn wish to do so, they can then trade on their holdings of the loan stock to yet other investors. These transactions have nothing to do with the company's funds since the company only receives cash *once* – from the original issue of the loans.

More about Share Capital

After their issue in return for capital (cash) to run the business, equity (shares) can likewise be bought and sold among other investors – again, however, the company does not get more cash.

Redeemable shares are generally not known as a method of financing since a reduction in the share capital of a company usually requires the permission of the High Court, to avoid the possibilities of fraud being perpetrated against the remaining shareholders.

Deferred shares (of which there are very few examples) have no rights to dividends until a certain level of dividends have been attained by ordinary shareholders.

The last point to note about **share capital** is that, generally, accounts will show two figures for share capital in the Notes which accompany the accounts. One will refer to **authorised share capital** and the other to **issued share capital**.

The distinction between these is that a company's authorised share capital (what the shareholders have said that they are prepared to see in issue) must equal or exceed the number of its issued shares.

Only the shareholders of a company can raise the number of authorised shares – not the managers of a company (unless they are the majority of the shareholders too, of course). In large companies, it is not unusual for shareholders to delegate that authority, within certain limits, to give the management discretion to use shares for opportunistic acquisitions rather than to have to come back to shareholders every time they want to acquire a small company. This liberty is also often allowed to the management of the company so that they can offer share option schemes to senior employees.

The next heading in the Balance Sheet after the subscribed share capital is **'reserves'**.

Reserves consist usually of three elements: **share premium**; **retained earnings** and, less commonly, a **revaluation reserve**.

The **share premium account** represents the difference between the nominal value at which shares were issued and the actual value that they were issued for. So, for instance, Company X might issue 1,000 shares of 10p each at a price of £1. It would raise £1,000 by doing so, but the share capital would be only £100 (1,000 shares at 10p each); so £900 of the amount raised would be credited to the share premium account to make plain that the whole £1,000 of actual money subscribed is represented on the Balance Sheet.

There are strict rules governing what can be done with this share premium account. It can be used for defraying the cost of raising capital, for instance, and certain bonus issues can also be made out of share premium.

The section called **retained earnings** or simply **Profit and Loss Account** is just that. It is the pot into which all the post tax profits, after payments of dividends have been made, are poured each year. It represents the cumulative total of the 'surplus' earnings of the company since its inception. If there are losses overall in an accounting period, these will have the negative effect of reducing the retained earnings. In listed companies' accounts you will often find that there is a separate line which shows the accumulated value to shareholders of the 'Profit and Loss account'.

Although dividends can be paid out by a company which has made a loss, they cannot be paid out unless there are sufficient retained earnings to cover the cost of the dividend. In other words, there have to be 'distributable reserves'. A dividend payment in the absence of such cover is a reduction in capital and is consequently fraudulent. Reductions in capital can only be made, you will remember, after they have been approved by the High Court.

The **revaluation reserve** represents the positive difference, or surplus, between the most recent (usually professional) valuation of all the Fixed Assets and the value at which those assets were placed in the Balance Sheet. The basic rules for valuing assets, you will remember, require that these assets be held at the lower of cost (less accumulated depreciation) and their current market value. But here one accounting rule conflicts with another as far as the presentation of the Balance Sheet is concerned.

Prudence would require that the accounts show a sum that equates to the lower of cost and realisable value for the Fixed Assets. But continually to ignore the increase in value that land and property usually experience would be seriously to undervalue a significant asset in the business's books and to understate the value of those assets to shareholders. So this would be ignoring the requirement to show a true and fair view.

This requires that proper, realisable, values be ascribed to assets. So any surplus that the assets can command over their book or written down value (which takes into account depreciation) – and which will appear in the values ascribed to those assets – has to be put somewhere on the *other* side of the Balance Sheet if the accounts are still both to balance and to show a true and fair view. The Revaluation Reserve is where you will find this balancing amount for the 'additional' value that the Fixed Assets possess over and above their written down value.

Unlike the share premium account, companies cannot make any form of distribution from the Revaluation Reserve. This is because, unless/until the asset(s) are sold, no actual money is available.

You may also find more esoteric categories of reserves – most of which are so rare as to be not worth describing here since they will usually be dealt with in the company's own 'Notes to the Accounts'.

However, one that you may come across more frequently – especially in stable businesses – is the **Capital Redemption Reserve**. The law requires that shares may only be redeemed out of distributable profits or the proceeds of a new issue of shares. When the repayment is out of distributable profits, English company law requires that the company must create a Capital Redemption Reserve. This reserve can then only be *distributed* in a liquidation or a Court approved capital reduction scheme but it can be *capitalised* through a 'bonus issue' of shares to shareholders. This means that existing shareholders get their shareholdings credited with shares which they did not have to pay anything for directly. So you can look upon it, effectively, as allowing ordinary shareholders to participate in the benefits of paying back other classes of shares. The example below shows the mechanism:

Starting position:

Share Capital	£
Ordinary Shares	100,000
Redeemable Prefs	50,000
Retained profits	55,000
Total	205,000

The Redeemable Prefs are redeemed by the company using the retained profit reserve (and by taking the cash from the other side of the Balance Sheet). Both of these therefore reduce by £50,000 and a Capital Redemption Reserve is created at the same time:

Share Capital	£
Ordinary shares	100,000
Capital Redemption Reserve	50,000
Retained profits	5,000
Total	155,000

Remember that the prime characteristic of share capital is that it is permanent. The Capital Redemption Reserve now represents a sort of phantom share value that is not 'owned' by anyone. So to restore the effect of the requirement that the share capital be permanent, and because there are still sufficient reserves so to do, the company gives ordinary shareholders a 1-for-2 bonus for their existing holdings. This is demonstrated below:

Share Capital	£
Ordinary shares	150,000
Retained profits	5,000
Total	155,000

The purpose of this reserve is therefore to prevent the total of share capital and non-distributable reserves from being reduced when some form of allowable share capital is repaid. To make this as clear as possible, keep in mind that all the forms of share capital are carried on the same 'side' of the Balance Sheet – so you cannot simply reduce one of them without putting something in its place to ensure that the whole thing still balances. If you simply remove the Redeemable Pref shares in the example above and show that they have been removed by taking them out of the Balance Sheet through the reduction of the reserves, then you would be double-counting *by reducing capital* at the same time!

Chapter 12:

The Balance Sheet: Terms and Definitions – Liabilities Side

*Asset value
*Goodwill
*Fixed Assets
*Current Assets
*Current liabilities
*Prepayments
*Accruals
*Long-term liabilities
*Provisions
*Net Assets

So much for the share capital side of the Balance Sheet. The other side – the assets side – also has its own peculiarities about which we have to be clear.

Firstly, you should note that the assets will also allow for the liabilities that the business has to bear, and that these are deducted from the value of the assets which has been previously indicated in order to give the **Net Assets** employed. Do not confuse this term, in this context, with the **NAV** (Net Asset Value) which is usually quoted on a per share basis and is described in Balance Sheet Ratios in Chapter 20. They are two aspects of the same thing, admittedly, but used in different contexts.

The usual starting category for the assets tabulation is **Fixed Assets** – which are usually divided into 'land and buildings' and 'other assets' – and this will be made more plain when you look at the appropriate Note to the Financial

Statements. Intangible assets are also listed here. The values for all these items are *after* depreciation (amortisation for intangibles – see page 127) has been taken into account. (Intangibles are amortised largely because it offends the principles of good accounting practice to retain something that has a subjective valuation permanently on the Balance Sheet.) Look carefully not only at the total depreciation charge for the period but at the depreciation and amortisation policies for each of the latter items since they will almost certainly not all be the same, and you should bear this in mind when you come to think about the charge for the forthcoming year. Freehold land is not normally depreciated (although mineral rights usually are) but certain types of buildings may be.

Investments that the company has made will also appear in this part of the Balance Sheet. 'Investments' will include **interests in subsidiary or associate companies** – with the investment showing at cost (less any amounts written off) plus the share of the retained profits and reserves of the associated company attributable to the investment – rather than the more conversational usage of the term to mean temporary investments in shares. This section will be very useful in enabling you to understand the structure of the business. Subsidiary companies are those in which the parent company has a majority stake; associate companies are those in which it has between 26% and 49%; and all other holdings are regarded as simply investments. Joint ventures will be in this section, of course, since the holdings in the joint venture vehicle will be an investment.

Here, before we leave the subject of fixed assets, intangible assets and investment, we have to introduce a rogue element into the discussion – one which is almost as much misunderstood as depreciation. That element is **goodwill**.

Goodwill is an amount for an intangible, a notional thing of some purported value to the business, like a brand, or a trading reputation, or simply a premium over the actual asset value paid in an acquisition, whose worth is probably subjective and judgmental, rather than hard and factual.

We have already seen that the fundamental point of a Balance Sheet is that it *must* balance. The only times that a Balance Sheet will not balance is when either a) someone has made an error in calculation; or b) a business has taken over another business and has paid for the acquired business more than it got back in physical (tangible) assets.

This last occurrence greatly upsets the principles on which Balance Sheets are set up. And since they are creatures of tidy habits, accountants will display a Balance Sheet that does not match as if it did, by *inventing* a number to place in one half of the accounts as a make-weight to bring about a balance. They do this either by incorporating a negative assets number – which would show that the liabilities exceed the assets and that the business is bust and shouldn't be trading! – or by showing a figure for goodwill.

I shall return to goodwill in Chapter 21 to investigate some of the liberties that can be taken with it by the unscrupulous – or the desperate. But for now, the definition that I have given above is sufficient to explain its purpose in the Balance Sheet – it is effectively a make-weight, a lump of numbers added to make one side of the Balance Sheet balance with the other.

Following the Fixed Assets come the so-called **Current Assets** – the ones that are essentially temporary in nature.

Into this category fall the value of **stocks and raw materials** and part-finished goods; **debtors** – the amounts owed to the company by its customers; and any **cash** that the company may have on deposit or on hand.

Debtors may sometimes be split into short term (payable on demand) and long term (falling due after twelve months). It should also be made clear which of these sums are receivable for trade and which are **prepayments**. The latter are payments that have to be made in one lump but where the benefits are spread over a period of time – for instance, annual insurance and business rates payments may fall into this category.

Debtors which remain unpaid at the end of the year should have a bad debt provision applied to them if it seems that they are unlikely ever to be paid. This should be disclosed in the Notes; the reserve is held in the Balance Sheet and, if the bad debt becomes a reality, then the cost is taken through the P&L account. Some Management accounts may well show a running provision for bad debts in the P&L, rather than keep the reserve separated in the Balance Sheet. They then adjust the P&L account at the end of the accounting period.

Stocks are not depreciated; however, stock is subject to the 'prudence' rule of assessing the lower of cost and realisable value and may be written down accordingly. Cash is subject to no valuation process since cash is cash, full stop.

After Current Assets come **Current Liabilities**, which are then netted off the Current Assets figure to give **Net Current Assets**. The current liabilities comprise creditors of less than one year's length – **short-term creditors**. These are essentially trade creditors, in other words, suppliers. Among them will be **accruals**. These are the reverse of **prepayments** and show where the business has received the benefit of something but not yet paid for it – so examples would be electricity or telephone charges, which are usually paid in arrears.

You will also find in this section the value at the Balance Sheet date of the **overdrafts** that the company runs. The borrowings should be split out from the trade creditors so that they are both clearly visible. It is also quite common to find **dividends due** but not paid and **tax due** but not yet paid among these short-term liabilities.

Following the accounting convention, creditors' figures are usually denoted with brackets around them to show that they are negative numbers – in other words, that they count against the total of the business's value.

The current liabilities could theoretically be required to be repaid at a moment's notice and so their size – and the direction in which they move – is a critical component of the Balance Sheet.

(Many Balance Sheets will indicate at this stage a subtotal of **Total Assets less** *Current* **Liabilities**.)

Set out separately from the current liabilities will be the **long-term liabilities** – usually just called **creditors** – which comprise loan stock owned by third parties or long-term loans provided by banks. This money is not 'at call' which is why it is kept clearly separated from the short term 'on-demand' loans.

Before you reach the final **Net Assets** line, which will 'balance' with the total of shareholders' interests (**Shareholders' Funds**) that follows further below, you may also come across a heading for **Provisions** under the long-term liabilities. Provisions mean amounts that the business has 'reserved' or 'provided' against assets because there is some doubt as to their true worth – for instance, bad debt provisions or provisions against a contract that may turn out badly. In Statutory Accounts, these are kept here on the Balance Sheet in the section covering Liabilities and Charges. In Management accounts bad debt provisions may show as a set figure lopped off the running total of profit until the end of the year – when they are adjusted to the actual value for the period. Provisions in listed companies' accounts are usually only disclosed as Notes to the Accounts unless they are very substantial, when they are taken as 'exceptional items' on the P&L.

Working Capital

It is useful to introduce at this point that the amounts for debtors, creditors – which operate in different directions as far as cash is concerned, of course – and stock, of all types, are collectively called the **Working Capital** of the business.

Chapter 13:

The Sources and Uses of Funds Statement

The third leg of the tripod
Sources and Uses and Cash Flow strictly defined are not the same
The components of the Inflow side
The components of the Outflow Side

The third leg of the tripod needed for the proper analysis of accounts is the Sources and Uses of Funds Statement, sometimes also called the Sources and Applications of Funds Statement. For simplicity I shall refer to it as the 'S&U'.

Unlike for the Balance Sheet and the Profit and Loss account, there are no new definitions to be introduced in any of the terminology used in the S&U. This is because the S&U does not contain any new concepts beyond those already encountered. The S&U is a hybrid – the offspring of the P&L and the Balance Sheet. It synthesises the information already available from the two other legs of the accounts and uses their terms to display something more.

However, there is one common misconception which must be dispelled from the beginning. The first thing to say about the S&U is that it is *not* a cash flow.

This gets *really* confusing when you come to large, quoted companies that have now adopted the terminology 'Cash Flow Statement' for what smaller businesses call the Sources and Uses of Funds.

A true Cash Flow Statement (usually abbreviated to Cash Flow) is a micro-management tool much beloved of bankers and those involved in planning businesses. It is never seen other than in documents that are confidential to a business and will never form part of the information that is readily available to the outside investigator. A true cash flow sets out – period by period, whatever those periods have been chosen to be – the components of the inflows and outflows of a business's cash, so that the net predictable bank balances, plus or minus, can be determined for the end of each period.

Obviously, the final period of our definition of true cash flow shows the end position for the whole sequence – and in that sense the Cash Flow Statements in large companies' accounts do resemble 'proper' cash flows that track the movements in funds period by period.

However, the change of name from S&U is probably only modification of something that described quite well what it was about – a definite case of 'progress' making life more difficult!

Because of this you have to deal with the Cash Flow Statement in the accounts of large companies a little differently from a straightforward S&U. Look at Appendix 5 for more detail on this. The fact that they are slightly different in format doesn't really matter, of course, since the techniques of breaking them down to look at what went on in the year will be exactly the same as for the simpler, non-listed model. (In fact the PLC model goes into greater detail – in such a way that less comparison is required to be done by the analyst – although probably at the cost of unnecessary detail being illuminated for the less sophisticated user.) The terms used will be largely the same and, if you can follow the format outlined here, then the listed company format should pose no problems when you come to look at it. Listed company accounts are also supported by another table called the Statement of Recognised Gains, which is dealt with at Appendix 5.

So, let's get back to analysing the S&U format that readers are probably most likely to encounter in looking at unlisted businesses, which illustrates the principles by which this part of the accounts are constructed. There is an example S&U in Appendix 3 which you may find helpful to follow as we go through the various stages. It is important to appreciate that there is no rigid format to the order of an S&U which must be followed, and therefore the listing order below may not be the one that will be encountered in any one set of accounts.

The S&U shows quite simply what its name says it will show; that is, where money came from and where it went. It is a sort of bridge between the Profit and Loss account and the Balance Sheet and links them by showing changes in the way a Balance Sheet is made up from one accounting period to another. Right at the very beginning of Section Two, I described the S&U as being like the drive-train of a clock that transfers the energy of the mechanism (the P&L) to the hands of the clock face (the Balance Sheet).

It does this by revealing some of the individual components of the Profit and Loss account and converting movements in profit into movements in cash or cash-bought assets.

The S&U also shares another characteristic with a Balance Sheet in that flows coming in have to balance flows going out.

The S&U is in many ways the most valuable of all the three accounts elements and at the same time probably the least understood by the layman. This is unfortunate since it is a primary component in any evaluation of the trend line of a business. It is a confirmatory tool and will provide the verification of suppositions based on examination of the P&L or Balance Sheet alone.

The format set out below is the most transparent to use. Unfortunately, you may well find other formats adopted according to the particular preferences of the accountant compiling them. These alternatives are not wrong, as such, but do not display the information so clearly as the method used here. If you do come across alternatives, the differences will probably be in the treatment of borrowing (added or repaid) or of funds raised to pay off borrowing.

The Inflow side

Although it may look daunting, the format of the S&U is quite straightforward. It starts off with the **Sources** of funds:

1) The profit (or loss) made by a business in the period under examination. Sometimes this may be shown at the operating (or pre-finance) level with interest (received taken away and charged added back) identified separately; the purpose of this is that it aids forecasting – but few published accounts will show the information this way;

2) Any extraordinary items that have to be taken into account will appear next: losses will be added back and profits taken away from the inflow. Exceptionals will already have been taken into account in arriving at the pre-tax total. (Such costs are discussed at page 99);

3) Adds back the (non-cash) depreciation charged in the period in arriving at the final pre-tax number (hopefully a profit, sometimes a loss) in the Profit and Loss account (remember depreciation is not cash; go back to Chapters 8 and 9 if you are unclear about this);

4) Adjusts for any proceeds from the sale of assets, depending on whether the sale was for more than the fully-depreciated value and is a profit on disposal (in which case the amount is negative or _taken off_ the inflow) or for less than the fully-depreciated value and is a loss on disposal (in which case the amount is positive and is _added back_ to the inflow). These counter-intuitive movements are best thought of as being adjustments to depreciation;

5) Adds back any (non-cash) amortisation of other assets like brands, goodwill, or intellectual property (which

means spreading the cost of those assets – a bit like depreciation);

6) You should also find that any other external sources of finance are identified in this section – if the business has received any government grants they will be shown here, for instance.

If there have been any share issues during the period under examination then the proceeds may also be added in to the pot. But no account should really be taken at this stage of **any** increase in borrowings if complete clarity is to be maintained, although styles can vary considerably according to the preferences of the person producing the S&U .

The number that is arrived at after all these apparent contortions is the total inflow (or **Total Sources**) – or the amount of money that was actually available to the business in the accounting period.

This amount must be balanced by (or equal to) the total of where all the money went – which is calculated principally by taking the difference between the values of Balance Sheet items at the start and end of the accounting period.

The Outflow side

The outflow or **Uses** side mirrors the inflow side in terms of the process of adding and taking away movements to produce a net outflow. However, a few more mental contortions may have to be gone through since there might be negative movements which have to be taken away; this sometimes means that you will be adding things back (since two negatives make a positive) when you might think you should be taking them away.

The first outflow item to be dealt with concerns the Working Capital required by the company: the amount of money used in paying for raw materials and other stocks taken together with the money due to come in from sales.

These figures, then, are the values of *changes* in debtors and creditors and *changes* in stock. (The American terms for debtors and creditors – receivables and payables – are really much simpler to use than the British ones but, since they are still not in common usage in this country, the reader is probably best advised to continue to grapple with the unhelpful British terms since these are the ones that will be encountered in looking at actual accounts.)

Changes in these values are calculated by looking at the difference between:

1) The value of the debtors at the start and at the end of the accounting period – in other words, in annual accounts, the difference between the figures shown for this year and last year, both of which appear on the Balance Sheet. (This will be a *positive* number if sales have been funded by the business through offering credit to its customers, since the business will have used its own cash to help its customers; and a *negative* one if credit levels offered to customers have been brought back.) However, if turnover fell during the period under review then there may have been a fall in the amount of credit offered by the company and so it is possible that outstanding debtors will have reduced. Check against the turnover line to see what looks most likely.

adding to that

2) The difference between the value of creditors at the start and the end of the period; a *positive* number if the company has had to use more of its own money to pay off creditors and a *negative* one if it has managed to buy extra goods and services through greater use made of its suppliers' credit terms – that is, using more of its suppliers' money to fund its own business

and

3)   The *changes* in stock holdings between the start of the period and the end of the period.

All these figures are taken from comparing the Balance Sheets between one accounting period and the next. There is a lot more to say about the significance of these movements and what they imply for the business, later on, in Chapter 22, which deals with the practical effects of the S&U in detail.

After these calculations, the amounts that the business has paid out in capital expenditure (increasing or replacing its physical assets) and making payments to shareholders – dividend payments or redemptions of shares, for instance – are taken into the calculation. Any tax payments actually made in the year in question – but not VAT – are added to conclude the calculation of the outgoings.

It is very important to understand that the payment of tax in the accounting period shown in the S&U is not the same as the tax charge that is shown in the P&L. The latter is the charge that will be paid (based on the P&L) for the year in question; the former is the cash sum that was actually paid during the period under consideration but for the previous year.

After this may come a line showing any money spent on acquiring other businesses.

The concluding figure for this calculation then is the total outflow (or **Total Uses**) of funds. If this is smaller than the Net Inflow, then there will have been a surplus of cash; if it is greater, then there will have been a deficit.

Some S&Us end at this point, if they incorporated cash movements and changes in borrowing in the body of the Statement. The statement ends up with a balanced total where both the inflow and the outflow will equal each other. A far better arrangement – in that it identifies the amount of extra cash that the business may have had to fund from either borrowings or new issues of shares – is for the S&U next to isolate movements in cash to show whether available balances went up or down. A net inflow or outflow will be visible. Then there can be no mistake which way cash went.

A surplus will result either in increased holdings of cash or a diminution of bank borrowings (or both) for the company, while a deficit will result in bank borrowing increasing or cash diminishing (or both). In themselves these are not good or bad things but their impact depends on the context of the business's development and the trends in its history.

To evaluate these trends properly, you need to have a run of information available so that you can see the course that the business has followed over a period of time and make an assessment of the influences that have been acting upon it.

This cannot be done, though, without an appreciation of more of the detail behind the individual elements that go to make up each element of the accounts – the P&L, the Balance Sheet and the S&U – so that you can see how some of them come about, and see the problems in recording the facts and the abuses to which that exercise is prone.

Having done that, you can go on to look at how the information available to the researcher can be utilised. Then you can look at some of the additional sources of information that are available and how they can be used to supplement your interpretation of events to give a rounded picture – but still a conjecture – of what is going on inside a business. As a first step in the right direction, I shall focus on some definitions next.

Chapter 14:

The Effects of Definitions

The ways in which defining things affects their impact on:
*Cost of Sales
*Depreciation
*Tax and dividends

Items in the Profit and Loss account can have a consequent impact on the Balance Sheet according to the way that they are defined.

It should be apparent – even at this early stage in your examination of a set of accounts – that if one thing is taken from another to give a final amount, then the size of the thing being taken away can have a crucial effect on the size of what is left.

This is particularly important when you look at how stocks, cost of sales and profits are handled in accounts; and when you consider the impact of depreciation on profit.

Costs of Sales and Stocks

The higher the value of stocks at the end of the accounting period, sometimes the higher the level of apparent profitability. An example should help the explanation of this:

Suppose two identical companies in the same sector both have sales of £100 million. Both companies start the year with opening stocks of £10 million and both purchase new stocks to the value of £15 million during the year. At a simplistic level the cost of sales is calculated by taking the value of the opening stock, adding to it the value of purchases made during the year and then deducting the value of the closing stock plus any attributable costs associated with that stock. So if Company A decides (as it is allowed to if it can justify it to the auditors) that its closing stock is worth £20 million (since it has added labour value to the stock in some way) while Company B decides that its stock is worth £15 million, then the companies will report very different profits for the year. Company A will report sales of £100 million less Cost of Sales (10 + 15 – 20) to give a Gross Profit of £95m; while Company B will report sales of £100 million less Cost of Sales of (10 + 15 – 15) to give a Gross Profit of £90 million.

Using this or a similar quirk of definition is one of the ways that mischief can be made with accounts – as we shall see in Chapter 18, Costs and Mischief.

Depreciation

The lower the charge for depreciation brought into the P&L, the higher the profits will be, and the higher the value of Fixed Assets in the Balance Sheet carried forward to future years (and the higher the overall value of that Balance Sheet) will be. Depreciation charges can be lowered by disposing of assets and not replacing them, or by altering the length of time over which an asset is depreciated.

Tax and Dividends

Most investment analysts are concerned with **PbT** or **Profits before Tax** on the P&L account which, as we have seen on the P&L, takes in everything, including interest charges on borrowings, before the final figure is struck.

Since forecasting tax is not required for most assessments of investment value, analysts will generally forecast down to the PbT line (of the P&L) in their predictions and merely go on to apply a 'notional' or theoretical tax charge when calculating the **eps** – earnings per share.

A company, on the other hand, has to show in its Statutory

Accounts what it thinks the tax charge will be. It also shows the cash amount of dividends that it plans to pay out for the year.

But what you might find confusing is that the tax charge and dividends shown on the P&L are not quite the same as the amounts for tax and dividends shown under these headings in the S&U.

Dividends shown in the P&L are the amounts that have to be paid out of the year's profits. In the Balance Sheet they will be held as the final amount proposed by the company's board. In the S&U they will be the cash amounts paid out for the final dividend last year, which wasn't approved by the company's shareholders until after the year end, and the amount actually paid out in cash terms at the interim stage of this year. Once again, the final dividend won't be paid out until after the conclusion of the current accounting year so it doesn't figure in these accounts as far as the S&U is concerned.

The tax position shown in the P&L will be the assessment of the tax due and will probably not have to be paid for at least six months – depending on the dates of the company's financial year. So the amount of tax that is actually paid out is the sum shown in the S&U. This will be the total of the amounts that are due, apportioned by the times when they were due to be paid. For the purposes of most analysis it is not necessary to re-calculate the figures that are given in the S&U, and any forecasting that you may attempt will be sufficiently broad-brush that it should not need to be obstructed by an attempt to make a detailed prediction of tax payable.

Section Three

Chapter 15:

Analysing the P&L: First Steps

---

*Piecing together information
*The battle between statutory and business requirements and the
  desire to conceal private information
*Remember time
*Seasonality
*The first piece of Analysis using two pieces of information to
  produce a third

To most people 'accounts' probably means the Profit and Loss account.

This is because the P&L is the dynamic part of the set and, although in some ways more complicated than the Balance Sheet, it is probably fundamentally easier to grapple with than the Balance Sheet – at least at a simplistic level.

This chapter will take a look at some of the components of a Profit and Loss account and show how by looking at them in a different way – perhaps slightly more critically – it is possible to find out how a business is behaving. There is not much number work to do from now on. There is greater concern about ways of thinking about things rather than the numerical mechanics of the accounts.

Subsequent chapters will look at the P&L in more depth and then we shall look at the details of the Balance Sheet and the Sources and Uses in the same way.

But before we start to look at individual elements there are two areas we should set as a background. These are

1) The way that you piece information together from the accounts to provide you with yet more information – so that what you end up with is greater than the sum of the parts; and
2) The way that you can extract information from what is available to you by bearing in mind that accounts are prepared to represent a period of time.

Piecing Together Information

Auditors and accountants have been treading a very thin line in writing accounts. They have had to find a middle way between living up to their statutory obligations and, at the same time, trying to satisfy the likely desire of the management and/or the owners of a business to conceal as much as possible from competitors and predators.

While companies have to reveal certain information by law, they also want to give as little away as possible to competitors about their methods. In preparing Statutory Accounts, auditors are mindful that they are serving both the public interest (in revealing information) and the interests of the company for which they are working (in keeping discreet and hidden as much as the law permits).

The current Statutory Accounts format is the result of a long battle that has stretched over a century and a half – since the time of the first Companies' Act – between those, usually the outsiders, who have wanted to reveal the goings on in a business to the wider world, and those, usually the insiders, who have wanted to keep as much of their business as private as possible.

On the other hand, Management Accounts are a crucial tool for managers to use in running a business. They want to know as much as possible about everything – often including non-financial information. I have seen Management accounts which included, as a matter of course, information on weather patterns so that the managers could measure the performance of their business year-on-year taking into account variations in sunshine!

The result of this continuing battle has been that, whilst the accounting profession as a whole has pursued the need for transparency and completeness of disclosure, individual company accountants want to tell you as little as possible while still complying with their legal obligations. The result is that considerations of discretion usually win, provided that the obligations of the law are observed. Consequently, it is usual in publicly available accounts for no more information to be given away than is absolutely necessary. This is the reason that Statutory Accounts and Management accounts differ so much in the amount of information they reveal.

So, given that the companies and their auditors have pared the real information down to the bone, don't waste anything that you do come across! Every part of the accounts has a potential value to you in building up a picture of what is going on. Discard nothing. You might be able to link two or more pieces of apparently unrelated information to gain an insight into what is really going on.

Remember, what you are doing is like building a jigsaw puzzle. The shapes of most pieces don't fit immediately. But later, you will find a use for them, and they will go on to give you an even better platform from which to tackle the next chunk of the puzzle.

I have already suggested that it is not enough to look at a P&L in isolation from the other elements of a set of accounts if a rounded picture of what is going on in a business is to be achieved. This means that there are other dimensions to the evaluation of a set of accounts which have to be considered to give more than a superficial view of a business's health or progress. These dimensions go beyond simply linking the P&L into changes in the Balance Sheet or appreciating how the S&U bridges the framework tentatively established by the other two components.

Once you have grasped that a set of accounts requires all

three elements to help you see the true picture, you have to make the next step, which moves analysis from the static to the dynamic, and involves thinking about movements *along a strip of accounts*. This means following one element of the accounts through year by year (or, even better, half-year by half-year) so that you can see changes in these components. You have to begin to think of a set of accounts not simply as a two-dimensional affair set out on a piece of paper but as a multi-dimensional puzzle that has depth and breadth to it as well, set out in a number of dimensions.

One of these dimensions is time.

Time – the 'Stream' Factor

Accounts are prepared to cover a period of time – usually twelve months as we have seen – the end point of which is often chosen for some careful reason. For instance, it may be that the end of the business's accounting year coincides with the conclusion of a busy period in the business's own commercial calendar; or it may be that the year end is a favourable time for cash balances for the business, which is not necessarily the same thing, or it may simply be the end of the tax year.

Whatever the reason, it is usually the case that the decision has not been taken arbitrarily but that there is some purpose behind it. The analyst or researcher should ask himself which reason it might be, since the correct reason will give some background clues to the environment in which the business operates – times of year when there might be surges in business; times of year when things might go quiet; large changes in stockholdings and cash requirements in consequence of any of these. For example, many retailers have their best trading period around Christmas and so choose a year end around January/February, or possibly even March when they can also take into account the New Year sales.

The answer to the year end question will also provide indications of factors that can be eliminated or considered when the trends of the accounts and trading are being reviewed over a longer period of time. Suppose that you know, for instance, that there is always a large cash balance at the end of the year and, one year, there is no such a balance; you can find no reason why there should not be from looking at the Balance Sheet and the S&U. Then you may have a clue to the way that the business was trading at the start of the new accounting year – a year for which you will possibly not yet have hard information.

If there is no immediately obvious reason for the year end timing at which you can guess, just hold in mind that few things in life are done without purpose – especially those as important as accounting properly for profit and therefore tax! – and wait and see what might turn up as you delve a bit further into the business.

One of the ways that accountants and auditors are able to conceal information is to collapse time to a simple period of so many months, a half-year or year, with the result that there is (usually) very little indication of what may have happened between the start date and the end date of an accounting period. Of course, the end date of one set of accounts is the start position of the next – so it may be possible to see a pattern if consecutive sets of accounts are compared.

Such effects are particularly marked when a company's cash position is considered. A simple – unsophisticated – examination of its accounts might suggest, for instance, that a company has a positive cash balance throughout the year. It ends/starts one year with a positive cash position and ends up twelve months later with a positive amount of cash that isn't much changed on the starting position. So did the cash stay the same all through the year?

The answer is that, if there is an interest charge, then it's more than likely that, at some point during the year, the company eliminated its cash balance and borrowed money on which it paid interest. This gave rise to a charge for interest in the P&L. This gives you a clue, then, to the pattern of trading that the business faces, since you can – by a process of trial and error – approximate the period of time and/or the amount by which it went into overdraft. You do this by making guesses about the amount of time that the company was in the red in terms of cash, and using the prevailing rates of interest that banks would have been charging for overdraft, until you get close to the amount of interest shown as paid in the accounts. For example, if you see an interest charge of £10,000 in a P&L when the company apparently has positive cash balances at the start and the end of the year, you might speculate that it went into the red for either six months at an average of £200,000, or for three months at £400,000 (assuming the interest rate it might have had to pay to be around 10%).

Further examination of the accounts might lead you to believe that this pattern of trading might be a regular occurrence.

If, on the other hand, cash balances are no higher at the end of the second year than at the beginning of the first, it is likely (in the absence of an interest charge or any other reason) that there is no marked 'seasonality' to the pattern of a company's cash flow, and that cash flows in – and out – at much the same rate throughout the year.

However, if there is interest charged against the company's P&L and you compare this with what it might be on the average cash balance throughout the year (as deduced from the Balance Sheet by taking the debt at the start of the year, adding to it the debt at the end of the year and dividing by two) you may be able to do some reasonable guesswork. If the interest paid is very much different from what you believe it should be given prevailing interest rates – either much lower or, more likely, much higher – then it is a fair bet that there is quite a large movement in cash at some point in the year.

Since companies usually organise their year ends to show off their best cash balances you can probably make a reasonable guess, if you see this sort of effect, that there is a point during the year (concealed in the accounts by the flattening of time) when large amounts of cash are required by the business which it cannot itself generate. It then has to borrow these sums from outside in the likelihood it will be able to pay them back later on in the year.

Going on from this is stepping forward a little too fast, so, for the moment just note what we have done.

1)   We have established how to use a P&L item to verify a speculation about a Balance Sheet change.
2)   We have also seen how two sets of accounts can be used to give us a confirmatory check on the effect of time on the changes in accounts.

We've used two pieces of information to give us a clue about the behaviour of the business that we could not otherwise have extracted from the accounts. In other words, we've just completed our first real piece of analysis!

So we are now beginning to use a set of accounts as a complete, integrated whole and to think of the accounts as giving us information from the stream of time that they truly represent, rather than in the jerky, step-like movements that they appear to display.

Chapter 16:

Analysing the P&L: Problems with Turnover

---

*The need to ensure consistent definitions
*Some problems with definitions illustrated
A practical example – the Acrow case

First things first: always read the small print! Before you start looking through any set of accounts read the accounting definitions that every set of accounts must carry. It's boring but it's essential. It is the accounting equivalent of making sure that the map is the right way up when you navigate in your car. You nearly always find these 'Accounting Policies', as they are known, written out just before or at the beginning of the Notes to the Financial Statements.

As we shall see, different sets of accounts often apply the same words to mean different things and it is essential to know which sets of definitions are being applied before you embark on navigating your way through the accounts – otherwise you might find yourself in the accounting equivalent of Timbuctoo when you wanted to be in Iceland!

The supposition throughout this chapter and the ones that follow is that the Statutory Accounts of a business show most of the information in which an outside researcher is likely to be interested. That may not be the case, of course. If a company is very small (so it is, by definition, private and its shares are not freely traded) it may choose to take advantage of provisions of the law which excuse it from even having to disclose its turnover in its Statutory Accounts. Faced with a company like this, there is very little that an outside investigator can do if the management of the company are not willing to disclose information on a privileged basis.

As you know, the turnover line is the top line of the Profit and Loss account and, not surprisingly, it shows how much the business 'turned over' during the period to which the accounts relate.

What this should show is the amount of the particular goods and/or services that the business deals in that it sold during the year. In practice, it can mean something quite different. The reader of accounts has to bear in mind that the definition of what turnover actually is will vary, like many other apparently simple concepts, from business to business. The only way of being reasonably certain of what the accounts' authors meant when they calculated turnover is to check in the Accounting Policies section of the accounts.

There are, in fact, good reasons for this apparent capriciousness on the part of the accountants. (Capriciousness is perhaps the wrong word, since accountants are probably the least capricious profession in the world – apart from actuaries, that is – most of whom decided against accounting as a career because it was too exciting.)

Through long practical experience, accountants have recognised that, although to apply the same rigid definition of turnover to all businesses might seem fair on the face of it, this is in fact grossly unfair as a way of attempting to show a true and fair view of what is happening to a business. A 'true and fair view' is the Holy Grail of accounting; the trouble is, like the real Holy Grail, it probably does not exist.

So, for the sake of practicality, they have settled on a compromise solution that effectively says that turnover can be (almost) whatever the business and its auditors agree upon, provided that:

1)   The definition is provided for the world to see and
2)   It is applied consistently from one period of time to another.

However, this does not prevent either quirks of definition from cropping up or the application of unscrupulous smokescreening (what some people might call downright old-fashioned cheating). Let's look at a few examples.

A business like a corner sweetshop probably does not have too much trouble working out what its turnover is: the number of sweets sold multiplied by their prices during a given period of time will give the cash value of turnover. It is comparatively easy because the sales are (usually) small in monetary value, carried out in a fairly small period of time and transacted with one, or perhaps two, customers at a time.

But what about a major firm of civil engineering contractors which builds bridges in remote areas in developing countries – projects which take many years to complete using United Nations' grants? How does it calculate its turnover? Or, how does an engineering business, which sells capital goods worldwide through a chain of linked companies in each of its sales territories, account for turnover?

The short answer is that there is no right answer to problem cases such as these two, and so Accounting Policies have to set out with considerable care what it is that the companies' accountants have sought to measure and what the auditors have sought to verify. Then the game starts to get more complicated and thereafter problems arise. All you can do is be aware of some of the tricks that may be employed in an attempt to flatter turnover.

The contracting company discussed above will probably take as its measure of turnover the amount charged to customers for work physically completed during the year on the bridges that it is building. That's fairly straight-forward. But what happens if it has associated companies which are jointly owned with local residents which are the ones that are actually completing the work? Then what share of their turnover does it take? And what happens if the contractor is supplying goods and services to those companies to enable them to do the work but hasn't been paid by those companies at the conclusion of its accounting year – still less received a dividend from them on profits that they might have earned (which will be accounted for separately, of course)?

You can see that the picture can get very cloudy indeed and that to take the turnover always at face value could lead to a very misleading assessment. Yet the accurate recording of turnover is crucial because turnover is the prime determinant of profit. An example may help illustrate some of the difficulties.

Acrow, a public company, managed to improve profits for thirty straight years by playing around (quite legally) with its turnover until the construction depression of the 1980s sunk its ability to do so. Acrow manufactured a wide range of capital goods and construction machinery. It carefully managed its turnover by using a network of associated companies through which it sold exclusively into different territories worldwide. Since these were associate companies – in which Acrow had a minority stake – the accounting rule governing sales meant that stock was lifted from the books of the parent company and transferred to the books of the associate. There was no doubt therefore that a sale had taken place and profit on it was duly recorded by the parent company.

However, Acrow's own agreements with its associates meant that these sales could be reversed after the parent company's year end if the individual associate couldn't bear the load. The goods themselves would then be redistributed, by being sold on to another associate where the local construction industry was in better health.

The system lasted from the end of the Second World War (when Acrow was established) until the worldwide recession of the eighties when every territory saw simultaneous localised problems in construction and these worldwide manoeuvrings could no longer take place. Eventually Acrow succumbed.

Acrow's management and accountants did nothing wrong or illegal in their transfers of goods, or in the way that they accounted for turnover or calculated profit under the rules that existed at the time. But that didn't stop the gullible from believing that the company could continue to defy the laws of physics long after it should have been apparent that its sales practices were morally bankrupt. Nor did it stop some newspaper tipsters from continuing to promote Acrow as a wonder stock, because of its 'unbroken record of growth', long after the professional broking analysts in the City of London became wise to the practice and it should have been obvious to all that the company would end up going out of business.

Chapter 17:

Analysing the P&L: Costs

The problems of one and many
High and low margins – the clues that they can give
Rising falling and static margins
How far do you go in looking at costs?
Extraordinaries and Exceptionals

Of all the elements in the Profit and Loss account, the costs section is the most open to error, confusion or downright manipulation in the construction of the accounts. This chapter will deal with the basics of the problem and the next chapter will go on to explore some of the mischief to which this can give rise.

Although the names and the definitions vary between accountants and economists, there are essentially two types of cost that are shown in a company's accounts:

1) The **Cost of Sales** – the costs of turning stock into sales; these are sometimes known (usually by economists) as the *direct* or **Prime** costs

2) The **overhead costs** – which are really everything else – the costs that have to be borne as a consequence of making or doing something. These *indirect* costs are sometimes split into fixed and variable costs (again, usages that are favoured by economists) and split into 'selling' (or 'distribution') and 'other' (or **general administrative**) costs by accountants. Service businesses of course effectively have only overhead costs.

Cost of Sales/Direct Costs

It does not take much insight to see that, if there are lots of potential definitions of what something may (or may not) be, then the scope for misunderstanding or alteration of what that thing actually is can be considerable. This is a significant problem since one of the primary signals of a business's intrinsic value is the level of *direct* costs that it has to suffer. This is because the level of costs that have to be borne can give a clue as to whether it is a price-taker or a price-maker. If you have to choose between the two, then the latter is the better one to be.

Another problem for a business with high *direct* costs is that direct costs take a long time to alter whereas *indirect* costs *may* be more amenable to management action.

The difficulties of calculating the direct costs of a business are made more difficult by the effect of the sheer number of transactions that take place in a business. When a business starts off it may be relatively easy to work out what the costs of one transaction are. Later, there may be very many transactions – and labour time and raw materials can be subject to some form of what economists call a 'benefit of scale'. This means that there is increasing operational efficiency as the volume of production increases. So it may be very difficult to work out what an individual sale costs because the lower costs that go to make up the total can only be achieved if lots of sales are made.

To make this clearer, think about what happens if you buy lots of a given product. You would usually expect some form of discount on the price of buying a thousand against the price of buying one. But that discount is only given to you if you do agree to buy lots. For instance, if you buy five hundred bricks to build a small wall, the price per brick is going to be very different from the price you would pay if you bought two thousand bricks to build a much longer wall. This is because it costs the same – more or less – for the brick manufacturer to set up the facilities to make five hundred bricks as to make twenty thousand.

But, at the same time, the price of those bricks is only available to you if you are going to use a lot. And there is no sense in buying thousands of bricks and getting a reduced unit price if you really only want five hundred.

So, how does the business that is selling to you calculate the cost of its operations that it must recoup within the price you are charged?

For most companies any such specific problems are likely to be insignificant because:

1) Individual considerations usually get lost in the wash of a large number of transactions, with customers who, in total, can be relied upon to demand thousands of bricks or pins or boiled sweets or jumpers or... whatever. Over these large numbers of transactions everything will tend to average out; and

2) The choice is not usually between selling only one of something and several hundreds or even larger quantities of something.

However, it may give problems to businesses that have to quote for individual contracts on the basis of being set up for long production runs and large amounts of raw materials consumption. Effectively, this can reduce their own direct customers to a handful. There have been many instances, even of very large companies with big costing departments, being caught out badly when such a big customer has requested a slight variation in the standard product or when design changes during the production process cause changes to pre-calculated production times or raw material usage. The aerospace industry can show some good examples of this.

Cost of Sales – or *direct* costs – is the first category of costs that are encountered in looking at a Profit and Loss account. These costs – the costs of the raw materials and labour that are used directly in achieving turnover – are the prime determinant of whether or not the company makes a reasonable profit. The efficiency with which a business converts its turnover into profit is dependent on the efficiency with which it controls its costs.

Margins

The terms 'gross profit' and 'gross margin' were both covered in Chapter 7 and also in the examination of the P&L account in Appendix 1. Usually, the higher the gross margin percentage the better, since there is then more room for other costs to be charged and still leave a reasonable 'net' profit (or net margin) per item. The overall **Net Margin** percentage, which is also very useful to compare, was explained in **Definition 5**, page 38.

Generally speaking, businesses which turn over a limited range of fast-moving goods can afford to have smaller gross margins than those which sell only a few very highly-priced items. It is for this reason too that businesses which have to compete strongly for customers also tend to have lower mark-ups and lower gross margins than those where there is not so much competition.

That is why the mark-up on, say, designer wristwatches is huge in comparison with the mark-up on most foodstuffs. The jeweller can count on selling only a few watches in any given period, so those sales he does make have to cover the costs he has to bear during the time that he is not making sales. The supermarket executive knows that he can count on a fair level of business all the time and that he must price competitively if he is to attract customers.

In looking at a set of accounts to assess a business's worth or potential value, one of the things that the researcher needs to do is to see how efficiently the business can turn raw materials into profit. In other words, how good it is at controlling its other costs. This exercise cannot be done in isolation but has to be done in comparison with other businesses in the same sector and across different periods of time.

So, ideally, you need to find similar businesses of a similar size and perform a number of examinations of their accounts over time – assess their 'profit histories' as the jargon has it – to see whether the specific business that you are interested in is doing well or badly by comparison with its peers, or even 'could do better'.

While it is not possible to list every type of result that may be found, there are some general guidelines for the results that are likely from such an examination. Bear in mind that, if the same thing is happening to every company that you look at in any one sector, then the indications you are receiving are probably ones either of terminal decline if everything is declining, or some form of structural change in the economy if things are getting better.

1)   Margins Rising

This probably means that either a) the business is going through a period of expansion, and experiencing the benefits of scale that expansion sometimes brings; or b) that competent management is able to trim out costs internally from levels that had been allowed to get flabby; or c) that competition in its sector or local geographical area is dropping away.

It could also mean that d) the business has established some form of technical process that enables it to generate better margins than the competition; or e) that a fashion for the business's products has developed and so there is a commensurate rise in demand.

Finally, it could mean that f) there has been better utilisation of otherwise spare capacity after a period of under-utilisation, implying cyclicality in the demand for the business's products.

Whatever happens, margins do not rise for ever. Competitors will eventually discover what it is that propels another business's margins and will surge in to take advantage by copying processes or products.

2)   Margins Falling

This can mean that either a) management are getting sloppy; or b) the business is experiencing an adverse movement in its raw material or labour costs which it cannot pass on; or c) there is more competition in the sector in which the business operates; or d) the business has decided to 'buy' turnover consciously to stymie a competitor for strategic reasons; or e) the business is itself going through some form of decline.

Whether this decline is permanent or temporary can only be deduced from a run of figures, which may not exist, of course – yet. If everyone's margins are falling, then beware!

3)   Stable Margins

This may mean either: a) that you are looking at a stable, well-run business that has squeezed all it can out of its market place under very competent management; or b) it could mean that the business is a big fat plum, run by complacent managers, that is just ripe for some faster, nimbler competitor to take a pop at; or c) it could equally mean that they are never going to go anywhere!

Stable margin businesses – which may appear to be boring initially – can be just about the most interesting of all to analyse and invest in, since it is almost certain that there will be a development, sooner or later. They are perpetually on the cusp of something happening.

Other Costs

The recognised format for Statutory Accounts now requires other costs to be grouped into '**selling**' costs, alternatively called '**distribution**' costs, and '**general and administrative**' costs.

While this breakdown goes some way to being of use – in that it helps again to split large numbers down into manageable sizes – it still allows an awful lot of latitude. This is not least because to follow these definitions to their logical conclusion would result in an absurdity of work in recording information.

For instance, the 'costs of selling' in most businesses would certainly include a proportion of the telephone bills that the business pays. But the finance director who spends his time, or that of his staff, in trying to apportion those phone bills between Jason in Sales and Karen in Accounts to the last penny, needs his head examined.

So, instead of looking for the whole picture from one set of accounts, we have to fall back on the trusted method of evaluating a business – by comparing it with its fellows and with itself over a period of time.

Of the two forms of comparison, the internal one is likely to yield more benefit to the outsider. Variations between individual headings of costs are likely to be reasonably insignificant between businesses (as well as being extremely tedious to calculate and to analyse) and will be mostly meaningless anyway because the businesses will be set up in different ways.

Variations in individual costs over time within one business, however, are likely to reveal more about the way that managers are able to control costs and so give an insight into the ability of a business's management team.

And don't forget that management salaries and labour wages are part of costs. So an examination of what has happened to them over time will also give a good indication of where the management stand, and whether they are able to control their labour costs properly.

In fact, the salary levels of senior managers are of such significance that a special section is reserved for them in the Notes to the Financial Statements and they have to be disclosed in some detail. Study this carefully. Compare pay levels with those of other businesses in the same sector for it will give you a precise indication of what the business's managers consider themselves entitled to, through thick and thin. Make up your own mind whether they seem to be in or out of line with their competitors.

And while we are on the subject (although it is not strictly to do with costs) share options and other arrangements have to be disclosed too, so it's worth having a look out for these to see if the management have decided to take some of their remuneration in the form of rewards for future growth in the value of the Balance Sheet brought about by increasing profitability. That can be a good indication of their faith in the business. Similarly, when directors unload some or all of their holdings, it can also be an indication of what they think of the short-term future of the business – and changes in directors' shareholdings have to be recorded in the Report and Accounts.

Extraordinary and Exceptional Costs

At some point in your investigations of a series of sets of accounts you are almost certain to come across one or both of the above. Extraordinary costs are taken 'below the line' – that is, *after tax* is accounted for – while Exceptional costs are taken 'above the line' i.e. after the normality of costs are accounted for but *prior to the tax charge*.

In the interests of fairness I should point out that it is possible to conceive of Extraordinary gains and Exceptional gains but these are so rarely encountered that they are almost redundant concepts. The reason is simple: your Extraordinary loss is incompetence; my Extraordinary gain is astonishing shrewdness!

However, the use of extraordinary items was so abused during the 1980s that they are now virtually defunct as an accounting device – in the UK at least – and the description that follows is for completeness rather than an exposition of what is likely to be found in a set of accounts for a UK business.

The two categories, Extraordinary and Exceptional, which accountants use to pigeon-hole events that are highly unusual in the life of a business, are often the source of considerable controversy between the business and outside analysts.

Treating them as Extraordinary involves stripping the costs – of events that are seen as completely once-off occurrences or highly unusual events – out of the Profit and Loss account. If they are once-offs they can be regarded as 'extraordinary' to the life of the business. Examples of such costs might be: a) closure costs of a complete division; or b) costs of clearing up a major industrial accident; or c) the costs of pursuing a major fraud.

Exceptional costs are not so unusual that they will only occur once, but they may have unusual consequences.

Confusingly, you may also find that Exceptional costs include exactly the same sorts of things that have been listed above. This is because claims for Extraordinary status are usually rather more difficult to sustain. In practice, in many instances it would be a matter for the directors to propose that the costs were Extraordinary rather than Exceptional and then for the auditors – and finally the Inland Revenue – to agree the claim. Examples of exceptional costs might be the closure of part of a business or the costs associated with repairing damage after a natural disaster like a flood or a fire. They will be very similar in nature to the examples given for extraordinary costs.

In whichever category they may be classified, the main purpose of separating these costs out is to ensure that interpretation of the accounts is not clouded by the effect of events that present temporary distortion to the business's underlying profitability. There are three major objections to these devices from outsiders:

Objections to Extraordinary/Exceptional Costs

1) *Extraordinaries and Exceptionals can be Identical in Definition*

The standard defence to this objection is that they are not identical *in application* – so apologists for the use of the concept might say that, while some companies may close divisions as a matter of course, it happens so rarely for most businesses that it truly should be considered an Extraordinary event.

However, if plenty of other businesses in the same sector are still managing to trade in similar circumstances, then what was it that prompted the managers of the afflicted business to make errors that were so severe that they led them to pack up before everybody else? Or could it be that they are taking advantage of the accounting provisions to hide the future effect of their failures (by taking pre-emptive provisions against problem areas of the business) or – more likely – cleaning out the failures of their predecessors?

2) Frequency of Occurrence

While an event may be classed as Extraordinary the first time that it happens, *what do you do when it becomes a more frequent event?* Oil companies, for instance, seem to suffer oil spillages of their product with depressing regularity. While the spillages may be unusual, particularly for one company, are they then truly Extraordinary – or even Exceptional – events?

Some companies do make a practice of closing complete arms of their business to reapply the resources more profitably somewhere else. But are these then Extraordinary or Exceptional events? This becomes a matter of some seriousness in times of economic recession when lots of businesses are forced to review the profitability of their range of operations. In these circumstances what was once thought of as an Extraordinary event becomes a little less so by degrees, until it becomes almost run of the mill.

3) Abuse of the Concept

Whatever the definition, given half the chance an alert management team will *abuse the general concept* by throwing every possible cost into an Exceptional/Extraordinary pot so that next year's results will appear that much better after all the rubbish has been cleaned out. This is particularly the case in large organisations whose shares are traded on stock exchanges and where the path of the share price can influence either the remuneration awarded to the senior management, or even their continued employment.

Here you have a clue to the reason why all this effort is put into this exercise. Share price movements of publicly-listed companies are driven by changes in their P/E ratio – which is the number of times the earnings per share can be divided into the market price of the shares. Earnings per share are dependent on profit and, as you know, profit is critically dependent upon the costs that have to be borne by the company. So pushing extraordinary costs out of the profit calculation for the current year (if the management can agree this classification with the Inland Revenue) swells the earnings per share and reduces the P/E ratio, making the shares look cheap(er) and thus promoting upward movements in the shares. If these costs can only qualify as exceptional, the company has to take them on the chin in the current year but in the knowledge that the same benefits should then accrue in the following year.

So, despite the fact that accounts purport to show the underlying trend by eliminating these unusual events, it could also be the case that astute management will be trying to play the system and smooth out for their own benefit – directly or indirectly – the vagaries that afflict any business. Before you accept them at face value, think very carefully about what the accounts are intended to show when these devices are employed.

In the next chapter we shall look at how the accounting of costs can be distorted to the advantage of the reporting company.

Chapter 18:

Costs and Mischief

The four major areas for mischief:
  Stocks
  Costs
  Off-Balance Sheet financing
  Depreciation

Whole books have been written about how companies manage to flatter their accounts by manipulating their costs. The number of ways in which can this be done is bounded only by the limits of invention of the accountants and managers preparing the accounts.

It is not my purpose here to describe the intricate details of every trick of accountancy. Nonetheless, it is not possible to evaluate something properly unless you know about the flaws to which it may be prone – if only to satisfy yourself that there is an absence of flaws. What follows is a very brief description of some of the little jokes that can be played on the innocent in the preparation of accounts. It only gives an introduction to these, not a detailed description.

Some of the grosser infractions of accounting good taste have now been outlawed, by changes in accounting standards made in the 1990s, because their effect was too outrageous to be ignored or scandals arose after the consequences were discovered by the investing public, even though they may have been known to professional accountants and analysts for some time – like the Acrow case referred to earlier. In looking at a run of accounts you should still be alert to the possibilities of deliberate flattery, to make sure that a sequence of accounts records has not been distorted by the inclusion of a formerly legitimate practice which is now ruled illegal.

There can be no defamation of the accountancy profession in saying that standards of accounting and auditing vary greatly between individual auditors. Grotesque examples of manipulation can still be found in the accounts of private companies – some of which may be the subject of examination by readers of this book. Equally, in defence of accountants, it has to be said that an apparently easy task, like recording the performance of a business numerically, becomes horrendously complicated when the size of the business increases beyond a modest level. It is perfectly possible that two opposing views of how to account for something can be apparently equally valid in terms of method.

Now the philosophical background is out of the way, let's have a look at how some little japes can be played:

1) Stocks

Since costs are the prime determinant of profits once turnover has been won, they are usually the prime target of the manipulators.

The most common way of altering the impact of costs on the P&L in any one year is to change the way that stocks are accounted for. This is done by thinking of stocks (which are of course a Balance Sheet item) as a reservoir against which additional costs can be drawn off or pumped back.

Stocks must be counted at the lower of cost and realisable value in the annual stock take that forms the basis for the appropriate entry in the annual Balance Sheet.

However, to take an example in microcosm, if a package of screws has been opened and placed on a work bench ready for a piece of assembly work, it could be that they will be counted not as *stocks* but as *work-in-progress* against which the business's accounting definitions might rule that some profit percentage or labour cost might have to be applied. Similarly, stocks that have been allocated to a customer *but not physically despatched* might be mis-counted (or even deliberately classified) as stock, pure and simple, rather than as turnover. Using these examples does not mean they are the correct or even alternative treatments that may be applied to the problem; it merely serves to show some of the tricks that can be used.

However, using stocks as a reservoir of value to alter profits and the value of the Balance Sheet has two drawbacks: 1) it can only be done infrequently since even the most lackadaisical auditors would be very unhappy about the basis of accounting for stocks being changed too often; and 2) there has to be a good reason for it to be done.

Some of these good reasons are set out below.

a)   Inflation

When inflation was at much higher levels than at present there were lots of opportunities to consider the value of stocks very carefully; now, with low levels of inflation generally, there are fewer. But inflation will come back!

The usual way that bases of accounting for stocks are altered is to change the way that stocks are recorded as coming into and going out of the business. In non-inflationary times, most businesses would use up stocks of raw materials by taking the first delivered stock into the production process and working through the stock holdings like a queue. This is called FIFO stock usage (First In, First Out).

However, if the cost of raw materials or parts is rising fast, then a business might choose to use the Last In First Out method (LIFO). This will probably assist it in trying to keep its prices better in line with its future costs. It needs good stock records and the ability to raise prices to customers reasonably easily.

Because the most recently purchased (and therefore, during high inflation, expensive) stock component is used at every opportunity, the effect of LIFO ensures there will always be enough cash to pay for replacement higher-priced raw materials. It also produces a higher level of **Cost of Sales** for the P&L and, consequently, lower taxable profit than would be experienced under FIFO. (For a worked example of this, to make the mechanics plain, see Appendix 4.)

b)   *Altering Timing*

Another way of altering costs is to push them forward into next year's P&L. This is done by taking the costs attributable to part-completed goods out of the P&L and regarding them as part of the value of those stocks, rather than work in progress – thereby knocking those costs out of this year's accounting for the P&L. This can be done quite legitimately under accounting rules (and is in fact a consequence of the acceptable need for matching, as far as practicable, specific costs against related profits). However, it has the side-effect of placing a heavier burden on the Profit and Loss account next year, so finance directors must use the practice with caution.

A variation on this theme – playing with discounts – is illustrated by the recent example of the games that were played at SSL (the merged combination of LRC and the company responsible for the Scholl brands). Shortly after the annual results for the newly-merged company's financial year 2000 were published, it became apparent to senior managers of the company that sales of condoms were suffering a massive dive. Further investigation revealed that sales of condoms in the year just ended and reported on had been massively inflated by huge discounts that had been offered to wholesale customers by the company's sales force – but that these discounts had not been properly accounted for in the year to which they related. So turnover had been hugely exaggerated for that year as customers took advantage of cheap supplies. Consequently the stocks that they now held meant that they did not need to buy any further supplies for some time and current sales levels plummeted. The company was forced to issue warnings about its profits for the current year and a full investigation of the situation was commenced in order to report the true situation to shareholders.

The building supplies company Wickes had suffered from a similar problem some years previously as managers sought to improve their own remuneration and shareholding values by inflating sales.

The trouble with monkeying around with sales in any manner is that, because the Profit and Loss account and Balance Sheet are so intimately linked, it is not possible to alter only one component in isolation. If you alter one part of the P&L, then you have to alter something else in the Balance Sheet. The 'something else' almost always has to be stock since this is the only component that exists in both Balance Sheet and P&L, and sales (which is what the P&L is all about) have to come from stocks, either pre-existing ones or stocks newly bought in. So little lies get bigger every day when they are shuttled between the P&L and the Balance Sheet to try to equalise the effect of unsupportable changes in one or the other.

2) Costs

a) *Capitalising Costs*

Getting rid of costs entirely can just about be managed by what is euphemistically known as 'capitalising' the cost of development work – as raw materials progress to become saleable goods. At the risk of greatly simplifying the concept let's look at an extreme example. If a new freehold building is built by a company for its own use, then it might be possible to regard the *complete* cost as being a Balance Sheet asset rather than saying that the costs of the land and the bricks and mortar alone are to be added to the Balance Sheet. The actual building costs would then have been 'capitalised', taking them entirely out of the P&L and putting the whole cost of the building in the fixed assets section of the Balance Sheet (with the concomitant results of both adding to the apparent strength of the Balance Sheet and, at the same time, reducing the effect on the P&L).

There have been infamous cases of abuse of this practice – for instance, one of the causes of the Rolls Royce aero-engine business crash in the 1970s was the capitalising of development costs on new engines – and the scope for accountants to use this particular dodge is now severely limited both by tightened accounting regulations and increased vigilance on the part of the tax authorities.

b) *Reserving against Costs*

However, it is quite proper for the management of a business to look at the prospects for a contract and, if it looks more than usually uncertain, to take provisions (which are of course extremely generous in their impact) against that activity turning into a lossmaker and thus to rid themselves of potential embarrassment from costs for some years into the future. Bad debt reserves are one obvious way of doing this.

Balance Sheet reserves can also be used to manipulate the true costs of an activity by having, for instance, certain types of exchange losses written off against reserves specially created for the purpose. This has the effect of leaving the P&L untouched by adverse currency movements, with the Balance Sheet taking the strain of changes in currency valuations. And since the provision has already been created, no harm is done to the Balance Sheet by adopting this approach.

3) Off-Balance Sheet Financing

The use of off-Balance Sheet financing – where the costs of a subordinate activity never hit the main P&L at all – is a recognised method of limiting the exposure of a parent business to risks run by a minor activity. Again, the worst abuses of this process have now been curbed by increased disclosure requirements in publicly listed companies but it is still possible for private companies to use the screens of different Balance Sheets to reduce the visibility of some of their actions.

It is worthwhile noting here that private companies are often more concerned with their Balance Sheet strength than are PLCs, since this is the prime measure against which bankers lend money to private businesses.

What happens is this. The costs of a risky activity (both Balance Sheet and P&L costs) are shunted off from the company undertaking the activity (Company A) to be included in the accounts of a business in which it has a minority stake (Company B). This minority stake classifies the Company B as an **'associate'** rather than a **subsidiary** of Company A, which means that Company A can avoid having to include in its own figures the Profit and Loss account and Balance Sheet figures of Company B for its group accounts. Instead, it takes the dividends that it receives when Company B begins to make a profit and probably soon thereafter buys out the majority partner. The effect is that it only takes on Company B as a subsidiary when it has proved its worth. If there are no dividends because Company B turns out as a dog commercially, then Company A's P&L is never affected – although its Balance Sheet may suffer drains of cash if it has to re-fund Company B's activities.

The theory says that, if the business never works, then it can be cut adrift and closed down without any repercussions. Unfortunately, for the companies that practised and perpetrated the worst abuses, theory and practice did not always match. This led to a spate of scandals in the 1980s when the abuse was at its highest. The trouble is that all too often these minor activities had a habit of getting bigger and bigger and then dragging down the parent as contingent liabilities (such as cross-guarantees) added up. And since the problem was concealed by being off-Balance Sheet, shareholders did not know about these repercussions until it was too late.

4) Depreciation

Another fruitful area for mischief is depreciation – the charge against the P&L for 'using up' the tangible assets of a business. In a small business the speed depreciation takes place can sometimes justifiably be altered by changing the rates at which these assets are 'used up'. Consequently there is also great scope for manipulation of the depreciation charge in altering residual values of assets – so that, for instance, a Balance Sheet might appear to be stronger than it really is. However, the tax laws restrict the extent to which this can be done and it is rare to find large, well-analysed companies mucking about with depreciation charges.

Readers with an appetite for learning more about these tricks are advised to look at specialist accounting texts and business histories for further information. Moving on from the seamy side of accounts, the next chapter will consider how you can put the information contained in the P&L to good use in evaluating a business and its prospects.

Chapter 19:

Direct Comparisons and Ratio Analysis

The problems of comparing numbers from different sources

The need to use comparisons when evaluating a business – comparing year against year, company against company and company against the sectoral trends – is worth repeating.

Numbers mean very little in isolation when considering a business and only display meaningful information when they are compared with something more or less equivalent. Numbers are merely data; comparisons are *information*.

However, it can be very difficult to compare information unless some form of common base is used, since there is a danger of trying to mix apples with oranges to produce a valid answer. What you will get, instead, will be a jumble of oranges and apples, a numerical pudding!

In addition, carrying large numbers around in your head in order to try to compare them with other large numbers is an inefficient way of making comparisons. The solution to this problem is to use ratios – one number (or set of numbers) divided by another to give some indication of efficiency. Ratios can also be used to reveal information that might otherwise be hidden. Ratios really come into their own when they are used to compare two or more different things – these can either be companies or periods of time for the same company, for instance.

So, stockbroking analysts concentrate primarily on the prospective Price/Earnings or P/E ratio of the shares of a company. This is a valuable subject and is dealt with fully in

Appendix 6. They also couple their calculations of the P/E ratio with other subordinate considerations about a share, to make an assessment of whether they should recommend to their clients that it be bought, held or sold.

Looking at the P&L only, and starting at the top, **turnover per employee** will be studied to see if more income is being derived from the workforce – or, even better as far as the investor is concerned, from fewer workers (since that means less cost paid out in wages). Companies above a certain size are obliged to state the average number of workers that they employed during the year in the Notes to their Accounts, so for them this information is readily to hand for the analyst.

I have already discussed the **gross margin** – the ratio of gross profit to turnover expressed usually as a percentage. Comparison of the gross margin from year to year will be made to see if there are indications of improvements in the business's terms of trade or a deterioration in its market place. Minor changes in margin can have big effects on businesses so these should be carefully reviewed.

The proportion **of selling and administrative costs to turnover** will be reviewed year by year to see if the company is spending money on developing an administrative 'tail', or if it is costing more and more to achieve the same amount of turnover, both of which may be indications of a potential deterioration in profitability.

Interest charges will be examined to see if indications can be gleaned about the amount of money borrowed during the year. I noted in Chapter 15 that if the amount of interest paid is dramatically out of line (either way) with the borrowings shown on the Balance Sheet at the year end, it tells analysts something about the pattern of borrowings during the year.

The analyst will also look at the **pattern of results** that the company announces across the year. Companies with publicly quoted shares have to make half-yearly announcements of their results on a pattern which conforms very closely to their end-of-year announcements.

Although these announcements are unaudited and so cannot be regarded in quite the same way (some companies have an unpleasant habit of slightly re-stating their half-yearly figures at the year-end stage) they give a useful pointer to the likely result for the year and have their own unique value in providing the analyst with a sequence of information.

Putting the half yearly results against the year-end results and deriving the second half figures by deduction shows how the business actually performed during the second six months.

Turnover, costs and profit are all then displayed so that, over a long run, patterns begin to emerge of the way in which business was won during the year and of the way in which borrowings and economic changes impact on profit.

There are two other significant ratios which are P&L related which are of importance to the analyst. These are the percentage **growth rate of turnover** (and profits, for that matter) and **return on capital employed**. The growth rate is easily calculated by comparing one set of annual accounts with another – and comparing the interim results, too. The uses of this ratio are obvious since it gives the prime signal of the way that the company's market is moving.

The second ratio, slightly more sophisticated than the rest, the return on capital employed, is sometimes abbreviated to **ROCE**. This measure is simply the Profit before Tax divided by the capital employed in the business. Capital employed refers to the *total* amount of capital being used by the company as at the year end and so has to include, in addition to the amounts identified under the heading 'capital and reserves' in the Balance Sheet, *all* types of bank debt and other borrowings. (A more sophisticated approach would be to calculate an average from the two values at the start and end of the financial year.)

This measure indicates how successful the company is in terms of the money it employs in conducting its business. It is a critical measure of the success of the business's management, since low rates of ROCE suggest that the shareholders would be better off if the managers stayed at home and the money employed in the business was given to building societies to look after. The shareholders could then enjoy a higher return from the interest paid on the money at less risk!

Aside from these measures, further ratio building from the content of the P&L probably suffers from the law of diminishing returns. You can have a look at any measure you want but the amount of information that you will glean from it is probably marginal in comparison with the effort expended in collecting the information and performing the calculation. There is ample insight to be gained by using the ratios described above, in combination with those that relate to the Balance Sheet, which I come to next.

Chapter 20:

Balance Sheet Ratios

Net Asset Value
Liquidity
Gearing
The Quick Ratio
The Acid Test
Working Capital ratios

The Balance Sheet is the outcome of numerous individual transactions. As such it can tell the outside researcher a great deal about a business if approached in the right way. We have already described it as being like a clock face. And, just like a clock face if used in the right way, it can tell you a great deal more than simply the time; ask a Boy Scout about all the navigational information you can get from a clock face!

But in order for this to happen the Balance Sheet has to be looked as more than a slab of data. You've got to think like an analyst and think of the Balance Sheet along a strip of time.

You will probably find that this approach is aided by a concurrent look at the Sources and Uses of Funds Statement, switching between the two as you go along. Although, in the case of the S&U, information is less easily meaningfully broken into ratios, quick comparisons with it as you move through the individual items of the Balance Sheet will probably show up changes more satisfactorily than a simple comparison with last year's numbers by using the Balance Sheet alone.

The place to start is with the simplest measure of worth that the Balance Sheet can reveal, one which indicates the value of the business to the individual shareholder.

Net Asset Value (NAV)

The Net Asset Value is frequently used to check on the value of an offer for a target company in the event of a bid. It is usually quoted as 'Net Asset Value per share' (total **Net Assets** divided by the total number of shares in issue – or that figure adjusted for any known movements in the share structure) and is therefore similar in concept to 'earnings per share' which you can find detailed in Appendix 6. **Net Assets** were defined in Chapter 12. The number of shares in issue can always be checked among the Notes to the Financial Statements, which will also detail information about likely changes to the numbers of shares in issue.

If an offer for a company is pitched at a price lower than the Net Asset Value per share, then the existing shareholders would be giving away value if they sell their shares for the price being offered. (Although there may be special circumstances, of course, which mean that the calculated NAV per share is never going to be realised and so the offer might be worthwhile.) In general, however, the NAV per share can be thought of as a floor or threshold price per share which an offer for the company has to match.

Although it is the most commonly used ratio and has great value, the NAV per share is very specific in its application and doesn't tell you very much by itself – or about the way that the company might behave in the future. There are other more useful measures for this.

Liquidity

The amounts of cash (or debt) in a Balance Sheet are the next things that can be easily measured by means of simple ratios. Most outsiders will look at a Balance Sheet in order to discover one of three things they will want to know: 1) is the company a good bet for an investment? 2) is it a suitable partner to do business with in terms of being a good credit risk? and 3) is it going to continue to be these things?

All these revolve around the amount of cash shown in the Balance Sheet. Remember, businesses bank cash, *not* profits. Therefore all the primary Balance Sheet measures of analysis are concerned with liquidity.

Liquidity is a term that you will often come across in reading financial pages. Essentially its focus is either upon how close physical assets are to being turned into cash or how readily they can be turned into cash or, alternatively, upon the proportion of a Balance Sheet that is held in cash or near-cash.

A **highly liquid** investment is one that is very easy to turn back into cash – premium bonds, say, to take an example from the personal financial sector, are almost as good as money, even though they cannot be cashed overnight.

So, if an enterprise is highly liquid (has a high liquidity ratio) it means that either it has a lot of cash swilling around in it, or that it has assets which are very close to being cash (demand deposits, for instance) or which are easily turned into cash; or it can also mean that it has large stocks of goods which can quickly be turned into cash.

Conversely, an example of an **illiquid** company might be a property company with a large land bank. This can be turned into cash, but would probably take a long time to do.

Gearing

Aside from NAV, for most analysts, the 'gearing ratio' is the one that they would look at first while considering liquidity. Americanese has crept into finance-speak and you may sometimes come across gearing described as 'leverage'. This is almost an obligatory feature on the information sheets prepared by analysts for their stockbroking clients. Gearing is a very important concept which has applications in forecasting, too, so it needs to be defined.

Definition:

The **gearing** ratio displays the amount of debt in the Balance Sheet as a proportion of total funds used (that is, shareholders' funds plus the debt itself). A negatively geared company will have net cash in its Balance Sheet.

It is difficult to draw a firm conclusion about the absolute proportion of debt that is 'good' or 'bad', since everything depends on context and on the trend that is being followed. However, generally speaking, smaller amounts of gearing are better than larger amounts, while a complete absence of debt can be as much an indication of stagnation and opportunities missed as of upright financial management.

It would be very unusual to find a large company without any debt whatsoever. Equally, it would be very unusual to find a business growing and developing without taking on some form of borrowing, since very few can generate enough cash to satisfy their needs during other than modest expansion or have owners/shareholders with deep enough pockets to provide for all their cash requirements. However, many smaller businesses in 'steady state' may choose to run without debt if they can, so as to limit the risk that is faced by the proprietors, since small businesses will probably only be able to achieve a satisfactory amount of borrowing by tapping the owner's own capital as a surety.

When a company has a net cash position it is said – as noted earlier – to have 'negative gearing'. Few companies persist in this condition for long, since positive cash is usually the precursor to a purchase of another company or to some other form of expansion. Small business owners are unlikely to want to harbour cash in the business for very long since the owner will probably feel it is better in his pocket than anywhere else. Similarly, in the event that a larger company does hold cash for a long time, its shareholders will probably want to know why, since the chances are that the cash could be used more profitably by being put to work in another business. Or they may want to know why the company is hanging on to all that cash when it could be paying out dividends. Or somebody else's shareholders will also ask the same question and mount a bid!

Current and Quick Ratios

For most outside observers the thing that they most want to know about, after looking at the absolute and proportionate levels of debt, is whether there are going to be sufficient cash resources in the business to enable it to meet its obligations as they fall due.

This test is met by utilising two ratios – **the current ratio** and **the quick ratio** or **'acid test'**.

The current ratio simply divides the Current Assets (stock and work-in-progress, debtors, cash in hand) by the current liabilities (except debts falling due after a year) to see if the company could cover its obligations from the existing reasonably liquid resources of its Balance Sheet. The result of this arithmetic is to give a ratio: in the case of companies where assets exceed liabilities the ratio will be greater than one. In the case where liabilities exceed assets then the ratio will be a fraction or a decimal number.

A value of more than one is therefore acceptable under the current ratio test while a value of less than one suggests that there would be a problem if the company were to be called upon to satisfy its obligations very quickly.

The reason why debts falling due after a year are excluded is that it would not be legally possible for such creditors of the company to call in their debts on demand

– and therefore presumably without the business having some reasonable notice to make arrangements to repay.

However, this measure is not really very useful since, without the dimension of time and some information about trading terms, it is very artificial. For instance, the current ratio assumes that all assets are liquid immediately – but assigns no significance to how long it would take to convert stocks into cash.

Slightly more useful, then, is the measure which enables the analysts to see what would happen if there was a sudden call on the company's obligations and there was no extended period of time to convert stocks into money. This is the reason why the ratio is called the quick ratio – because it implies that there is no time to do anything other than pay what is due, simply to pay up *quickly*.

This ratio eliminates stocks from the calculation. Not surprisingly, there are few companies which can report a quick ratio greater than one; a ratio of around 0.75 would probably be respectable as far as an outside credit analyst would be concerned. It is also possible that companies that are able to meet this 'acid test' may well be very stodgy, conservative businesses or ones which are in decline.

However, just using either (or both) of these measures in isolation will give a very skewed appreciation of the business. At the very least, a run of the figures should be analysed to determine the way in which things are moving, and then that should be judged against what is known of developments in the company.

For instance, it may appear that the business is reducing liquidity year by year – but is this a matter of the terms of trade moving against the company (bad) or is it simply a matter of what was once free cash being applied to projects that will increase the rate of return to shareholders in the longer term (good)?

Halfway through building a jigsaw it may appear to show a recognisable pattern, but in looking at accounts the picture cannot really make sense until all – or virtually all – the pieces are in place. So beware of leaping to conclusions about the ratio of debt in the Balance Sheet.

Working Capital

As well as the ratios considered above, there are a number of combination ratios which utilise items from the P&L and the Balance Sheet and which will further illuminate a business's position. These are principally concerned with the Working Capital items of the Balance Sheet. As they concern the items that the business actually uses to operate, they can be very useful in compiling forecasts for the way that the business might operate in the future. A full assessment of a business's worth would take likely performance fully into account.

For businesses that make or sell things there will be a stock figure somewhere in the Balance Sheet. (Service businesses won't have any such figure. The only thing resembling stocks they are likely to have will be supplies of paper and other office materials. These may be referred to as stock but will probably be in the assets as 'office equipment'.) The value of the stock together with that of the debtors and the creditors combined (as described in Chapter 12) form the Working Capital of the business. If analysed comparatively and diligently over a period of time, this can show whether a business is expanding, contracting or static.

Stock Turn

One of the difficulties for any outsider in looking at a business is knowing whether changes in the turnover of the business are due to changes in the market place or changes in prices, or are just simply erratic movements. By using the average value of stocks (calculated from the start of the year and end-year values shown in the Balance Sheet) divided into the turnover for the most recent year, a measure of how fast the business is utilising stocks can be gained in terms of how long stocks hang or dwell in the business. This ratio gives an indication of the way that the business turns over its stock and this can be usefully compared with similar businesses. If carried over a run of years or reporting cycles, it also gives an indication of true growth (or otherwise!) in the business. Growing businesses turn over stock faster – all other things being equal.

Creditor Days/Debtor Days

Creditor days and debtor days are often used by outside analysts to give a clue to the efficiency of the business in collecting cash in from its customers and any potential cash-flow problems the business may be experiencing. Both these values are obtained by dividing the value of the debtors and trade creditors respectively by the value of turnover and then multiplying the result by 365. As we shall see in the next chapter, however, what they tell us must be treated with some caution since they can be fairly easily manipulated.

A value for creditor days of less than 45 suggests that the business is not taking advantage of normal trade credit terms (ask yourself is there a reason for that, such as taking discounts for prompt payment?) and a value for creditor days that extends substantially, over two analysed periods, suggests that something may be going wrong with cash flow.

Similarly, if a business has a debtor-day value that is much greater than 45 it suggests that it is being subjected to liberties by its customers. If debtor days suddenly and dramatically decrease, then that may be an indication of some sort of recent cash problem as the company put the squeeze on its customers to drag in cash (or possibly a change to some form of factoring or invoice discounting) as much as a general tightening of control.

Without going much deeper into the very exotic refinements of Balance Sheet ratios, you should be able to see that arriving at a conclusion about the situation of a business depends, once again, upon comparison. As with all comparisons using incomplete information, this has to be coupled with a degree of guesswork to see if there is a likely explanation that can be supported by further examination of the evidence.

Chapter 21:

Balance Sheet Mischief

*The year end date
*Cash manipulation
*Running down stocks
*Playing games with creditors and debtors
*Goodwill
*Games with Stocks

In the same way that you have to know what mischief can be done to the P&L, you have to have an idea of some of the tricks that can be played with the Balance Sheet if you are going to do a proper job of analysis.

Since the Balance Sheet shows the *result* of a trading period on the financial position of a company, rather than *movements* along the way, it is open to considerable abuse. To use a domestic analogy, anyone who has wall-papered a room will know that someone who watches the entire job from start to finish might have a different impression of how well the job was done from someone who only came in when the wall-papering was finished!

Balance Sheets are a bit like that: it is easy to make the results look better when you don't need to reveal exactly what happened along the way. Since the primary rule of Balance Sheets is that they have to balance, then, provided that they do, what happens to make them balance is – to the unscrupulous at least – rather more 'open to interpretation'.

The simplest way of flattering a Balance Sheet – with absolutely no funny tricks of accounting manipulation – is to choose a date for the business's year end when the amount of cash coming in to the business is at a maximum or when the amount going out is at a minimum.

The accountant can choose whether this cash is applied to reduce borrowings or to swell cash held in the bank but the effect will be the same. If the date is chosen with skill, then, no matter which of these is done – the first thing that happens is that the company's gearing ratio will be below the level it would otherwise occupy.

Three or four weeks later the position may be very different, as the business might by then have to pay out for raw materials for the new financial year's production requirements or have to begin a major investment in new plant. However, for a full year, as far as the accounts show, the company's Balance Sheet will benefit from the brief visit made to the company's bank account by the extra cash; and outsiders' records will show a gearing factor well below the actual (running) value.

The same effect can be achieved by running down stocks in anticipation of the year end. This has another double virtue – it releases cash that is otherwise tied up in unproductive stock, at the same time as reducing the drain on cash paid out to creditors in the future. There is a third virtuous effect to this process – cash coming in can be used to pay off old invoices, so keeping creditors happy and perhaps providing the temporary illusion that the business is stronger than 'normal' trading would otherwise allow.

Care has to be used in this manoeuvre, though, since too heavy a reduction of the stock level will leave the business dangerously exposed to stock shortages and possibly a liquidity crisis in the future as stocks would then have to be bought in volume at short notice to meet production requirements.

As a variation of this dodge, it is also possible artificially to improve cash outside of normal trading patterns, by having a sudden drive against delinquent debtor accounts, or by limiting the amount of money that is paid out to creditors at the year end, or by delaying prepayments of any sort.

However, since debtors are an asset and amounts due to creditors are a liability, the accountant has to weigh up whether he would prefer to see extra cash in the Balance Sheet or the **Net Current Assets** value at a higher level. It isn't possible to have both – or is it?

What about writing out a cheque to a creditor and entering it in the accounts as is the correct thing to do – but not actually sending the money out until after the conclusion of the accounting period and the books are closed? (This is, of course, strictly against the spirit of proper cash accounting.) That way the accounts reflect the change but the bank account stays fat, dumb and happy. Wouldn't that be a clever wheeze? Or what about doing the same thing for prepayments and getting another double whammy?

Cash is a fairly easy component to fiddle with. But profit-related items can also be cosmeticised. For instance, for nearly all businesses, bad debts are a feature of business life. It is an unfortunate fact of business life that some customers go bust and some dishonest individuals take products and then refuse to pay for them.

The prudent accountant will make a provision against bad debts as a matter of course and squirrel it away in the Balance Sheet. By using this provision judiciously, the effects of bad debts on the P&L can be smoothed and minimised, since the provisions in the Balance Sheet are adjusted and the P&L never feels the pain, while the damage will never affect the Balance Sheet much either. It is unlikely that any individual write-off will be of sufficient value to cause much grief and, anyway, the effect will be swallowed in the greater mass of the Balance Sheet as a whole.

Back in Chapter 12 I said that I would look at some of the tricks that could be played with goodwill.

Goodwill arises as an accounting concept when one business acquires or takes over another. Because of the need to tempt potential sellers out of their shells, it is usual for more money to be paid for a business than it can be technically proved to be worth. To make this plain let us look at an example:

A business has a Net Assets value of, say, £1m. That is to say that the value of all the assets less *all* the debts is £1m. All other things being equal, that will be a value at which the owner is indifferent as to sale or retention. To make him sell, something more has to be offered – say an extra £250,000 – which will represent the potential of the acquired business to the buyer in terms of, say, how much extra profit can be wrung from two businesses combined because of complementary product lines or filling in geographical gaps in market coverage.

However, in accounting terms, there is a problem. The credit and the debit side will not match in the acquiror's books: The acquiror will be paying out more for the business than it will subsequently be able to place in the Assets on its Balance Sheet to match the Capital and Reserves as increased by the price paid. This gives the accountants a headache. So they use the euphemism 'goodwill' to get around the problem by creating a balancing 'intangible asset', to record in the Assets on the company's Balance Sheet. This goodwill, normally the substantial majority component of intangible assets, is thus no more than a made-up value which, under English Company Law, has to be written off fairly quickly against its Balance Sheet value, or through the P&L so that it impacts retained profits at the end of each accounting period. This process is called amortisation rather than depreciation. The goodwill simply represents the excess paid for an acquired business beyond its proven or 'tangible' value. The best way to account for goodwill is not settled and there is a great deal of theoretical discussion among accountants about whether the write-off should be against past profits through the reserves, or against future profits through amortising the amount year-by-year – with a charge against the P&L which eventually translates through to the Balance Sheet.

This intangible is very much a subjective value. It is essentially derived from a price agreed in the final stage of purchase negotiations, and so there is much scope for interpretation in exactly how it should be treated. In particular, if a business can be regarded as merged with another, rather than acquired by it, then there is a much more favourable accounting treatment available for a number of other components of the Balance Sheet like reserves, dividends and, consequently, Net Assets.

Goodwill is a relatively rare thing to find in smaller companies' accounts because it involves the existence of substantial funds in order to be brought into being. Taking over another business is not a cheap exercise. It is more often found in the Balance Sheets of the bigger, quoted companies and, in consequence, the effects of the purchase of one company by another will usually be well trawled over by professional analysts. Furthermore, regulation of these larger companies is now conducted fairly rigorously, leaving little scope for markedly cavalier behaviour on the part of finance directors. The intricate minutiae of merger versus acquisition accounting can therefore remain outside the scope of this book.

So, where else can you look for mischief?

Perhaps the greatest scope for naughtiness is afforded by using stocks as a cover. Stock is the major item that appears in both the Balance Sheet and, modified as explained on page 51, in the P&L account. While the scope for manipulation of services companies is lower, because of having little or no physical stock, there is still some room for fiddling with the allocation of overheads to work in progress.

Even though the results of inflation are less of an issue now than they were twenty years ago, problems with the valuation of stocks in inflationary conditions give a useful insight into the effects of stock value changes on profitability. This is illustrated at Appendix 4. The value of stocks can be altered, either to inflate, or to diminish the value of a company Balance Sheet, and to inflate or diminish the Cost of Sales line on its P&L. This will either pad a Profit and Loss account or bolster a Balance Sheet.

Most companies only place a very terse statement in their accounts as to how they value stock beyond the required minimum basis (see page 67), so direct comparison of one business with another in this respect can be very misleading. If comparative analysis is to be worth anything then great care has to be taken by the analyst to ensure that the bases on which stocks are being accounted for between companies are broadly comparable; this should also be the case for accounts from the same businesses that are being compared year-on-year.

Chapter 22:

The Sources and Uses Again

What the S&U can do for you
How to analyse it
Cash Generation and Cash Consumption – the basic cases

Chapter 13 introduced the basics of the Sources and Uses of Funds Statement. We will now take things further by looking at the detail of the information that the Sources and Uses provides and how the S&U information can be employed in analysing a company's position.

You might like to look again at Appendix 3 while going through this chapter.

If you have got this far you will be fully aware that proper analysis of an individual business can really only take place if there is the possibility of analysing a run of information. This gives you a sense of the history of a business and from this you can begin to derive trends in the way that business performs.

You can also, of course, make a guess at certain possibilities by looking at trends in other businesses in the same market-place during the same period. This gives you a good background against which to analyse, but will not necessarily tell you very much about the special situation of any one business that you are looking at.

This is where the S&U comes into its own. The beauty of it is that (within the limits of the accounting conventions) it does some of the comparison work for you by showing the way that changes in a Balance Sheet came about from one year to the next. In doing this it has the additional virtue of revealing some more information about the business – because it shows the shape of changes that would be indistinguishable otherwise and, in doing so, it helps you to predict forthcoming changes.

The S&U helps provide answers to questions like:

What happened to the profits?

What dictated the size of the dividend?

How can there be a dividend paid even though there was a loss on trading?

What was the money from the rights issue used for?

How has the company managed to buy more businesses – by using cash or raising debt?

The answers that you will get will depend, of course, on the questions that you ask yourself when you look at the numbers in the S&U. The S&U – if analysed diligently – contains all the answers to questions like the ones posed above. For instance, you will be able to tell after analysing the S&U, in conjunction with the information provided in the rest of the accounts:

Whether cash went into buying assets or paying tax or dividends;

Whether the company is facing a year when it may find it difficult to generate cash again (if the surpluses of last year were due to unusually large asset sales or the raising of more loans or share issues, for example);

Whether a dividend, which looked unusually mean, was kept low because the management were aware

that there would have to be heavy spending on stock in the coming year.

From this you will see that one of the main purposes of the S&U (if not the main one, in fact) is to show where money went after the company generated it – as well as exactly how it was generated. Rather perversely, the top of the S&U is not always the right place to look for illumination about these crucial consequences. You sometimes have to start some way down the statement and then work your way around it. And you must always bear in mind the process of finding out the information from the entire set of accounts (see Chapter 6).

This means looking at the S&U in more than a mechanical way. Analysing the statement line-by-line should only be done after you have worked out what it is telling you overall.

So the place to start is to see whether the company generated cash or consumed it during the period that is being reported on. This may not be quite as easy as it sounds, since it can take some study to work out which way cash went depending on the format adopted. However, the format itself should be fairly easy to follow once you are familiar with the basis of what the S&U is trying to show you.

Whatever the format, there should be a net inflow/outflow line in the S&U which states the changes in net liquid funds. In the PLC version of an S&U this line is usually titled **Net increase/(decrease) in cash in the year**.

This is the line that you want to home in on since it tells you whether the company consumed cash or generated it. Once you have established that, you can move on to look at the components of the change.

It is obviously the case that cash will reduce if outgoings exceed income; and also that the reverse is true – that cash will be generated if less is spent than comes in. However, you want to know a bit more than that. Simply saying the company spent more or less than it earned doesn't get you very far in analytical terms. You need to know if that was a chronic position, or just a one-off, or the beginning of a trend.

There are four major ways in which companies can consume cash and four major ways in which they can generate it; not surprisingly, they are almost mirrors of each other. Once I have set out what they are, I shall go on to discuss each one in turn and indicate some further sub-divisions of each category.

Consumption of Cash

1) Trading losses are so significant that they exceed even the effects of depreciation added back.
2) Working Capital requirements increase substantially.
3) Assets are purchased.
4) Loans are repaid.

Generation of Cash

1) Profit levels are buoyant and, with depreciation added back, create a surplus over uses to which the cash is put.
2) Working Capital requirements shrink.
3) Assets of some sort are sold.
4) Shares are issued or further loans are raised.

Let's look first at the **Consumption of Cash**:

Trading Losses

Losses by themselves do not necessarily mean that a company will lose cash. This appears to fly in the face of reason but don't forget that the depreciation charge, which is knocked off profits in the P&L computation, is not a real cash item. It has to be added back to profit in the S&U to get the true cash-based position. This 're-injection' can make a huge difference to a company's cash position –

especially if the company has a large amount of machinery – what analysts call 'a large asset base'.

However, when losses are significant, or when the business's asset base is small, then the likelihood of a cash drain becomes greater. This is because a small asset base means low levels of depreciation which cannot act as a sufficient buffer against the cash effect of trading losses. So trading losses are much more likely to be damaging, in cash terms, to young businesses (which will not have accumulated much of a capital base) or to service based businesses where there may be little capital equipment.

Incidentally this is one of the reasons why trading losses at the 'dot.coms' hit them so hard. They suffered from the twin characteristics that they were young companies and had little capital infrastructure to cushion them.

The effects of trading losses will possibly be magnified unless management are alert to taking action to reduce Working Capital. This is discussed further below.

Working Capital Requirements Increase

Working Capital refers to a collective of Balance Sheet elements – stock (of all types); creditors; debtors. For the purpose of the S&U it can also mean dividends and taxes due.

When a company expands its business it may find that its Working Capital requirements outstrip its ability to fund them out of its own cash. This is nearly always caused by the fact that payments have to be made to suppliers before cash is received from customers.

A small business will usually find this is a temporary condition – unless the expansion is sustained and also requires the addition of physical assets (see *Assets are Purchased* on page 136). A larger business may find that the cycle will take much longer to right itself. This is because of the larger amounts required to expand an already large business and because the chances are that a large business will have 'lumpy' Working Capital requirements that cannot be easily altered except in large increments. Big companies often use lots of machinery that cannot be purchased in small amounts. By contrast, small businesses may use modest amounts of machinery which can be purchased in smaller units.

Similarly, an expansion of trade often means that the expanding customer base has to be funded – in other words, the amount of money outstanding from debtors increases as more customers owe larger amounts, perhaps for longer.

Expanding small companies sometimes find that there are also problems thrown up by a lack of control of credit to their customers as their resources get stretched. The effects of this can also send Working Capital rapidly spiralling upwards.

In addition, a company experiencing trading difficulties will often find its credit restricted. This means that it may have to find cash from somewhere else to pay suppliers. Once a company is in trouble, word usually spreads very rapidly and it is not long before suppliers start to rein in their credit terms. This makes the problems that prompted the initial payment difficulties even worse.

Dividend payments are a very unlikely reason for a desta-bilisation of cash in the accounts of a listed company – only a reckless management will increase borrowings to fund a distribution. However, there may be tax reasons for small private companies to do so, possibly connected with retire-ments, sales of shares or disputes between shareholders requiring some shareholders to be 'bought off'.

Similarly, a well-managed large company should never find that its tax position affects borrowings but a small, volatile, company may well find that the timing of its tax bill is unhelpful, especially when a poor year comes after a bumper one. Don't forget here that the tax actually paid by a company is different (in terms of the timing of its tax payments) from the tax charge that is assessed at the foot of the P&L (look again at Chapter 10 if you need to revise why this should be so).

Assets are Purchased

Companies often build up cash resources with the intention of embarking upon acquisitions. When an acquisition is made there will obviously be sudden, significant reductions in the cash available to the business as the 'war chest' that has been developed is expended. You will see this in the S&U as a decrease of cash resources and a countervailing increase in expenditure which should be identified as 'Purchase of subsidiary'.

Similarly, if the business invests in extending the amount of capital plant that it uses there will be a diminution of cash and a compensating line for 'Purchase of Fixed Assets'.

Loans are Repaid

In Chapter 11 I explained that one way of funding a business at the outset is to provide it with some form of loan capital. One of the distinctions between loan capital and equity capital is that loan capital is not a permanent part of the business's funding structure and consequently has to be repaid at some time.

The pattern of repayment is usually known from the outset of the life of the loan and so can be provided for in the company's financing plans. However, the repayments will nonetheless need to be shown as a purpose to which cash is put and will show up in the S&U as 'loan repayments'. It is possible – under one infrequently encountered structure for the S&U – that all repayments of all types of loan, including overdrafts, are shown as 'loans repaid' but this is rather too brutal for most purposes and it is normal for overdraft reductions to be shown separately.

Now we can return to the **Generation of Cash**:

Profit Levels are Buoyant

For a business that is only apparently making modest profits but which has a heavy asset base – an engineering company, say – most of the cash available to the business will come through as a consequence of the effects of the operation of the depreciation charge. The Profit and Loss account will have been debited with depreciation – thereby reducing the level of profitability. But profitability and cash are not the same thing, and cash will still flow through the business even if turnover is at a low level. Where the depreciation charge is high because the asset base is high, this can be quite significant. By definition, the amount of cash inflow will be broadly equivalent to the profit made, plus the depreciation charge, and you will see this if you look at the Sources and Uses (if there is a loss, it will be the depreciation less the loss, of course).

This may only be of modest comfort during times when orders are hard to come by. However, the silver lining to the cloud of low order books is that, since so much of the cash available to the business comes through the effect of 'retiring' some of what would otherwise have been profit into depreciation, it is possible for such businesses to run very profit-lean for a considerable amount of time, provided they have a minimal flow of cash sufficient to pay wages.

The effects of only a modest increase in margin can then have a very substantial effect on available cash resources when business picks up. There will be a dramatic increase in the amount of cash available. This partly accounts for the irregular growth spurts in cash that are often seen in small businesses in the engineering sector.

Obviously there has to be no substantial growth in any of the other facets of the company's spending pattern for there to be a surplus. But if a company is in a stable state, and in a market which is reasonably stable, then this can be quite a common experience. Most small businesses – after they get to a certain age – exhibit this type of characteristic since they will have stabilised their customer base, have a generally stable order book and not require vast sums for capital replacement.

In such circumstances, the major growth in outflows is likely to be in the remuneration paid to the manager-shareholders or the dividends to outside shareholders. That is, until the next problem is thrown up!

Working Capital Requirement Shrinks

This may sound good but it can also indicate some form of decline in the company's fortunes. A healthy business generally has either stable or modestly increasing Working Capital requirements, since this implies a market place that is either static or gently increasing in size.

If a company's Working Capital shrinks then it may be because the creditors' list has got bigger – which could mean that the company: 1) has had to test its suppliers' patience by not paying them in order to conserve cash; or 2) that not so much of whatever the company produces or sells is being sold and so fewer resources need to be bought in (don't forget that creditors' and debtors' cash movements usually work in opposite directions); or 3) that stock requirements are not so high – for similar reasons; or 4) that debtors have paid up what they owe and the customer list is getting smaller. It is important to grasp here that using suppliers' cash reduces the Working Capital requirement in cash terms just as providing credit to your own customers increases it. So you can shrink your Working Capital needs by using your suppliers' credit to fund your business – up to a point, that is.

A smaller Working Capital requirement could also be because the company was previously weak, having to pay up in advance on a 'pro-forma' basis to secure supplies. Creditors are now extending normal credit terms. It might be because the management have adopted working practices which have meant a one-off reduction in stock-holdings. Equally, it may be because too-generous terms previously offered to customers have now been reined back.

As you can see, without some form of supporting evidence from the rest of the accounts or the reports of the chairman and directors, or in a run of numbers from a series of annual accounts, it is difficult in isolation to tell what is happening.

You should therefore be alert to the range of possibilities that the numbers can suggest and treat the situation accordingly. Try testing a supposition, based on a sensible argument informed by the evidence of the rest of the accounts, and then see if your argument holds water, by looking at the accounts again to see if you can find holes in what you have suggested.

Assets of Some Sort are Sold

The only wrinkle that you should watch out for is if you are forecasting cash movements for the coming year. The sale of an asset – be it a single piece of machinery or a company – can have significant effects on the depreciation charge for the next year and you should look very carefully at the assets section of the Balance Sheet and the associated Notes to determine what the effect of the sale has been or will be.

Don't forget, either, that the S&U – like the P&L – shows the sum of all the events that have occurred during a year. Depending on the asset's sale date, it may well be that the accounts carry only half a year's depreciation for it, or two months, or eighteen weeks, or whatever. You will have to allow for this in making your calculations when you come to make forecasts for the coming accounting period.

Shares are Issued or Further Loans are Raised

It is sometimes the case that the S&U shows the opposite of what might be expected by the reader – an outflow is shown when a net inflow was anticipated or vice versa. This is in practice covered by the raising of additional capital, either as loan or equity but this should be shown separately in the format explained here. This can only happen if the two events explained in the paragraph below occur within the same accounting period.

An example would be that a company might decide to

purchase new equipment and raise money to fund it at the same time. The purchase of the equipment would be shown as an outflow, obviously. But it would be covered by the raising of the loan for the same amount, which should be shown separately, to produce a neutral cash flow position overall. The Notes to the S&U should identify this and the layout should be sufficiently transparent to ensure that what has happened is made plain to outsiders.

As noted further below, shares are rarely issued and taken up by shareholders unless there is a good reason. The reason usually has to be explained before the shares are issued; otherwise shareholders will baulk at parting with their money.

Unfortunately, the format of the S&U sometimes has the effect of disguising a share issue by using a device similar to 'netting off' so that the purpose to which the share issue was put absorbs the effect of the raising of the cash in the first place. (This is a problem very much resembling the one explained above of a company raising a loan simultaneously with the purchase of new equipment.)

This is not a sinister piece of duplicity like some of the tricks described in Chapters 18 and 21 on mischief in the P&L and on the Balance Sheet. It is merely a by-product of the structure of the S&U. It will not trap you if you are alert but it can make life tedious while you search for the piece of information that confirms what you already know to be the case. You have to make sure that your own calculations balance (remember the S&U has to balance outflow and inflow).

It is only rarely the case that a business is able to raise new capital (loan or equity) on the basis of an uncommitted use or an unstated purpose. Most shareholders or lenders will want to know the exact purpose of the cash-raising. Few providers of capital will make cash available for management to speculate. Occasionally, it is true, companies do raise cash with the specific intention of embarking upon a series of acquisitions, but it is generally a rare thing to find a company management entrusted with this sort of *carte blanche* by shareholders.

It may be, though, that the events of raising the cash and spending it on a set purpose are separated by the end of a financial year, and so, technically, the cash appears before it is spent, swelling the business's available funds. A note to the S&U or a reference in the chairman's or directors' report should always highlight this, if it does happen.

Chapter 23:

Other Sources of Information

Company Documents – brochures and catalogues
Websites
Shareholders' documents
Newspapers, journals, newsletters
Brokers' reports
Market reports and surveys
Credit agencies
The Courts
Company Visits and the AGM

I started this book off by encouraging you to think like an analyst. There is one more trick you must learn if you want to do that. The thing that distinguishes professional analysts from people interested in just one or two companies (apart from the experience that they have) is their wide knowledge of an industrial or commercial sector. By knowing lots about what is going on across a whole sector they are able to fix a benchmark for judging the worth of the companies that they look at within it.

Knowing only the details of the single business that you are interested in is not the best way really to develop an informed knowledge of what you are looking at. You can spend a very long time ploughing through accounts to find out what a business looks like and still not come up with much beyond a narrow view of the specific business you have been studying.

This will not help you very much when you come to look at predicting the patterns of trading or interpreting the strengths and weaknesses of the company in which you are interested. You will miss the wider picture if you concentrate solely on the view presented only by the accounts of the business itself.

In order properly to assess what a business is, what it is capable of and how well it might do in the future, you really need to get a rounded view of its wider prospects. This can only be obtained from information that is available outside the accounts of the company.

There are a number of sources of such information. Some are easily available and some less so. Let's start with the easy ones first.

Company Documents

If you are a shareholder of a publicly listed company then you must, by law, be supplied with the annual report and accounts of the company and any other important documents such as interim results, takeover circulars, notices of AGMs and so on. If you are not a shareholder, getting hold of listed company accounts is still very easy: you simply phone or fax the company's secretary for a copy.

The first port of call for official information on other companies registered in England and Wales (apart from the companies themselves) is Companies' House. This is the headquarters of the Companies' Registrar and is based in Cardiff. All companies must return their report and accounts and shareholder information to the Registrar annually. Copies of these documents can then be obtained from Companies' House. These can either be posted, or retrieved electronically. The Registrar has also sub-contracted to commercial enterprises like ICC (see below) certain services such as providing information to non-shareholders.

Apart from the obvious document – the accounts – another useful source of information is any sort of promotional literature or brochures produced by the company. These will give details of products and prices and possibly little snippets of corporate history that help make more sense of the company's current operations. By comparing prices and product specifications with those produced by competitors it may also be possible to gain a fair idea of whereabouts in the marketplace a company is trying to position itself.

Websites

Now that more and more companies are trying to sell their products electronically, a scrutiny of the website of a large company may reveal interesting facets of corporate life and culture. The extent to which companies use the web as a medium of communication differs markedly; some see it purely as marketing tool, while others publish information that investors will find useful.

A selection of airline websites shows differences in approach. Look at the BA website (www.britishairways.com), the Lufthansa site (www.lufthansa.com) and that of Delta Airlines (www.delta.com) for a taste of how different the purpose of sites and the display of information can be. And for a really good site with lots of corporate information try Ryanair's site (www.ryanair.com).

The liberation of information and markets brought about by the development of the Internet also means that there is a burgeoning availability of amateur analysis, comment and plain tittle-tattle that can be tapped. The best of the self-investment sites, like Motley Fool (www.fool.co.uk), have bulletin boards where novices can tap into the accumulated wisdom of more experienced company-watchers. Using this resource, it may be possible to find out the answer to the particular question that unlocks the understanding of some aspect of a company's operations. And if you don't know, you can post a question on the appropriate bulletin board and someone will surely offer an answer!

Many stockbrokers are also getting round to publishing information on the web and these sites can be very useful for the amateur stock-watcher, with a comprehensiveness and quality of information that is usually only available to professional analysts or at great cost to the layman.

HS Financial Publishing Ltd (better known as Hemmington Scott or HemScott) provide an extensive amount of information that can be accessed free of charge if you use them as your Internet Service Provider. Like the Motley Fool and other good sites, you can also establish a portfolio-tracking service for yourself to keep abreast of all the changes in your own holdings of shares.

Trawling carefully through the web with the help of a search engine you can also get a great deal of information about trends in sectors by tapping into specialist research sites. As part of the enticement to use a site more fully, many research companies give away some information in the expectation that site-users will find it so useful that they will enter more deeply into the site (and pay money for further services). Judicious use of these sites can provide you with a great deal of background information that you can piece together to get a wider picture.

If you can't find a site for exactly the company that you are interested in – which is going to be the case for the majority of small companies, of course – then think laterally and look for a site that is close to what you want and see what you can glean from that. It is surprising how much information can be gathered from general sources that will offer you a direct insight into your own particular target.

Don't neglect the newspapers' own websites. *The Guardian* (www.guardian.co.uk), in particular, has an excellent archive of its own articles that you can trawl through for comment and analysis. The FT.com site is also an excellent source of information from newspapers worldwide. You can download these at nominal costs if the information isn't freely available.

But, beware of all the information that you can find on the Net. The Internet's great virtue should be that it is largely uncensored – but that means that anyone can spread his views more or less indiscriminately or for an ulterior purpose. It is not unknown for unscrupulous individuals to ramp up a story using some of the flakier bulletin boards favoured by 'self-traders' to try to inflate the value of their own holdings in the shares of a company (or sometimes to get the price down) – so you must check what you learn from the Net against your own understanding. If something doesn't look right, then leave well alone.

Shareholder Information from the Company

The most significant pieces of information affecting shareholders' interests have to be communicated to them directly – and there are serious penalties imposed on companies and the officers of those companies who neglect this duty.

But by far the majority of information about companies in the UK – large companies that is – reaches shareholders through announcements to the London Stock Exchange, which are later reported in the financial sections of major newspapers.

Information has to be communicated to the Exchange first since this notionally satisfies the requirement that information has to be released to all shareholders and potentially interested parties simultaneously. In practice, this means that small shareholders are severely disadvantaged, since they usually lack the means to deal in the shares at the drop of a hat as can the professionals.

One thing you *can* do (for free) is tap the London Stock Exchange's own website which is regularly updated all through the day. This website is to be found at www.londonstockexchange-rns.com On it the announcements companies make can be read or downloaded within a relatively few minutes of their official release. This means that if you know, for example, the day that final results are due for a company you are keeping tabs on, you can be reading them almost at once and well before learning the best (or worst) in your daily newspaper.

Assiduous collection of information released to the Exchange can provide valuable insights into a company, since the significance of some information only becomes apparent after the event. For instance – although it is strictly outside the true scope of this book – details of **share transactions by directors** (which listed companies have to notify to the Stock Exchange) can provide useful clues to investors about the timing of their own transactions. There are very strict rules to govern share dealings by directors – but there are holes in the regulatory framework and some people do not have the high moral sense that should be expected of them in such positions. These transactions are regularly reported in the weekly *Investors Chronicle* and can also be found the day they happen, either through good websites such as those mentioned above, or directly from the London Stock Exchange website.

Clippings Files

A clippings file for the company(ies) in which you are interested, properly filed and indexed, can be a useful source of information to broaden your own understanding of a company's affairs. If you do clip information out of a paper, make sure that the date of the paper is noted on the clipping so that it becomes possible to store information chronologically.

Information from Third Parties

For many investors – professional or amateur – *The HemScott Company Guide* is one of the most useful publications. This book, which is updated quarterly, gives details of all listed companies and the performance of their shares. It details all announcements made by the company and gives brief commentaries of significant events. As a simple, readily-available supplement to the accounts for a company whose shares are listed, it cannot be bettered. In addition, HemScott produce a range of information for investors that can be very helpful in analysing companies against established ratios, including information on CD-ROM.

Most of the 'serious' **newspapers** have financial sections which cover movements in the share prices of significant companies and some – like the *Financial Times* – will also carry quite detailed analyses of company results which they will prepare from the views of stockbroking analysts and from talking to the company direct.

Even if you are not interested in these companies themselves, you may find it useful to collect information on them if they share a sectoral interest with a company in which you are interested. For instance, a major building materials' manufacturer may report quite extensively on conditions in its marketplace, which may be of interest to you if you have an interest in a smaller building materials' firm.

Newspapers also carry economic reports from pressure groups and by **specialist trade bodies** – like the Retail Consortium, the Society of Motor Manufacturers and Traders or the Housebuilders' Federation – and these can also be placed in your clippings file to help you in your assessment of the market place.

However, don't absorb information indiscriminately. As with everything else, you will find that a comparison of data over time will help you sort out the wheat from the chaff as far as forecasters are concerned. Some have a very much better record than others. And don't forget that official statistics are almost *always* revised upwards from the provisional information that is released initially!

For even more detailed examination of sectoral trends you might choose to use one of the **specialist sectoral reports** that can usually be found at good **business libraries** in major cities. Companies like Jordans produce regularly up-dated, excellent information on sectoral trends that is principally designed for companies' own marketing purposes (simply ask for the Jordans report at a local business library). The information that they collect is hard to rival – let alone beat – unless you are prepared to undertake some very costly and lengthy work yourself. Collected from the companies themselves, it is distilled into sectoral analyses with a commentary written by an expert and provides a very detailed insight into trading conditions within a sector.

If you get really keen on one particular sector then you

should think about subscribing to one of the plethora of **trade journals** that cover events in a particular industry. It is surprising how avidly these are read by professional stock-broking analysts. This is not because of the quality of the writing (or the incisiveness of the opinions!) but because these specialist magazines and papers are probably the best informed of all the observers of any industry.

They usually report the start of economic trends before anyone else and, even if they miss the impact on individual companies, the general trends are usually all that is required for astute observers to work out what might happen to individual businesses. This is invaluable for those following the fortunes of companies which have no share listing or only limited trading in their shares.

For companies where there is a public listing of the shares you might choose to read **investment papers** like *Investors Chronicle* or *Investment Week* or even to subscribe to a **specialist financial newsletter**. For this latter course you are going to have to be pretty serious in your intentions since, as these publications are not available across the newscounter and they make a virtue out of their low circulation, their cost is generally quite high. However, if you are serious, then they probably cannot be bettered as a means of finding out what is going on inside a sector or a business – if they cover it. You can get a good idea of the quality of the information these publications provide by asking for a trial copy (or copies) to be sent to you; so try out two or three and don't rush to buy the first one that you come across. For some areas – like the Alternative Investment Market in the UK (AIM) – though, the competition is fairly limited, with the sector being under-researched generally.

Commercially Available Data Banks

What happens if you want to know the details of a company's finances quickly but don't have access to the company's information yourself ? How do you go about getting the information?

There are a number of companies who have vast amounts of commercial information on tap and which you can get either through the post or electronically. **ICC Information Ltd.**, in particular, carries the details of the annual accounts of all British companies and many foreign ones on its database (www.icc.co.uk). Once you have established an account with the company these can be downloaded at will for later, more leisurely, analysis (but you do need to have special software to do so). The range of information available from this source is as much as the private researcher could ever need. Some simple analysis can also be purchased already done for you, if you wish.

Although much of the useful basic information about a company – registered address, turnover, list of directors – is essentially free, using the service in depth can be quite costly. But be careful not to request information that later turns out to be worthless for your purpose; many smaller, private companies take advantage of the smaller companies' provisions of the Companies' Acts and surrender only abbreviated accounts to Companies' House. You will find that these are virtually worthless for the purposes of analysing past trends or the company's current financial situation. If you see a section that says 'Modified Balance Sheet' on the ICC on-screen forms then you will probably find that there is little information contained in the file that will be worth paying for.

Indirect Information

Indirect information about companies is also extremely useful. Financial information isn't everything in analysis and in some cases what you really need to know is more about the products that the company makes.

Information about products is provided by publications such as **Kompass** (published by the CBI). This huge book covers every type of manufactured product you can think of (and some you have probably never heard of!). Its value lies in the fact that, if you are looking at a company for which there is no readily available comparison that you are aware of, you can go to Kompass, check the product code of the company that interests you and (probably) find a whole list of companies in the same area of the market place. You can then maybe analyse those to give you the comparative information you need. Even a negative result – no available competition – will give you some information!

Kompass also has sister volumes, published under the same name, for companies located throughout Europe, and there are similar publications available for the USA and Canada and Australia.

Sometimes it may also be of use to know if the company that you are interested in has any subsidiaries (or a parent or associated companies). Using **Who Owns Whom** (Dunn & Bradstreet) will provide this information and because of the organisation of the publication you can look at the company up (to see if it has a parent) – down (to see if it has subsidiaries) – and sideways (to see if it has any sisters) with equal ease.

Lastly, a series of volumes called **Key British Enterprises** (Dunn & Bradstreet again) provides mini-portraits of most of the larger UK businesses. While the coverage of this book is limited – because of the scope of what it tries to cover – it does give useful information, broken down by county as well as by type of business.

Other Companies' Information

It may be unnecessary to point out that the mirror of information about the company that you are interested in is information produced by its competitors. They will also produce price lists, marketing information, accounts and illustrated reports, and these can be used to build up a picture 'in relief' of the general business area. If you can find out information about a competitor you are half-way to building a picture of the target company.

Other Administrative Sources

If you use the ICC company information service, or one like it, you will find there is a reference to **'unsatisfied CCJs'** among the information you are able to look at. 'CCJs' are County Court Judgments – judgments made by a County Court against a company for non-payment of debts up to £5,000.

It is generally difficult to track down a record of CCJs by yourself since you have to know the jurisdiction in which each judgment was made to be sure of finding it. It is usually much less time-consuming and more practical to employ the services of a company like ICC.

Although largely toothless in themselves (since they are civil judgments, the state apparatus will not enforce them but will only help an aggrieved party to recover costs), they do have an important secondary function in that they indicate to third parties the credit-worthiness of an enterprise. Although mistakes occasionally arise and the system of recording judgements is far from infallible, take note of outstanding CCJs when looking at a company. They may indicate that something is very wrong if there are a large number of them clustered together or if the company has a chronic history of accumulating them.

You may be surprised to find that large companies often have unsatisfied judgements outstanding against them for apparently trivial amounts. This is because subsidiary companies sometimes attract adverse judgements. The trading morals of small subsidiaries may be less pristine than the image that the parent would like to portray, or disputes may arise more readily at a local level where small suppliers may be involved. In some sectors – construction, for instance – suppliers and principals have an all-too-ready penchant for resorting to litigation at the drop of a hat, especially when record-keeping is below the levels that might be expected of large companies.

If you are thinking about placing business with a company that you are looking at, then **credit checks** can be run.

The simplest method of doing this is to write to the other party's bankers and ask for a reference but checks can also be made through commercial credit rating agencies such as Dunn and Bradstreet.

Checks on individuals are regulated by the Data Protection Act and are not generally available to private individuals requesting data about someone else. However, it is possible to conduct some limited enquiries about businesses and individuals by consulting **Equifax** (www.equifax.co.uk).

Company Visits and AGMs

One of the best ways to understand any business is to see it in operation. There are probably few opportunities actually to have a tour around a business if you are a complete outsider but opportunities may occasionally be offered to existing shareholders. Some brewery companies, for instance, habitually hold their AGMs in their premises and then organise tours around for the attendees.

Company tours give the shareholder the opportunity both to ask questions and to see the inside of the business for himself. Although to be fair, there is likely to be little of significant use to the serious analyst in just being guided around a brewery unless there is also a chance to ask questions of suitable penetration as well. Generally these are not encouraged and you may well embarrass your hosts if the tour has been entrusted to an otherwise junior member of the management. However, if you are being shown round by, say, the finance director, then he has to be considered fair game!

Whoever takes you round, a chance to see the process of a business should never be turned down – unless you are an expert in the process or field already – since there are always new things to learn. And the very simple process of looking at how a business works can provide you with new insights into the detail of its accounts. Equally, there is nothing like a company tour to help bring the dull stuff of accounts alive!

Unlisted Companies

If you are a substantial but otherwise sleeping shareholder in a **business whose shares are not listed** there is no reason for you to be refused an occasional tour around and a chat with the management if you wish – although you may find that such visits are confined to times acceptable to the managers. These may be the best times to show off the business, of course!

You are quite entitled to ask for an explanation of the detail of the accounts during your visit. The insider trading rules and closed-season provisions which affect the trading of shares by directors of listed companies do not really apply to small companies, unless there is a fairly large number of shareholders who can actively trade their holdings informally. There is no real reason why there should not be a release of information to shareholders of small companies more or less on demand – except of course that continually to fuss about shareholders' individual enquiries may distract management from running the business.

However, managements of companies are often prickly about releasing information – for all sorts of reasons – some good, some not so good – and it is quite possible that you will not get much of a hearing for your questions except at the AGM, since the managers could well claim that to favour one shareholder with information would be unfair on the others (although, in a company where there is no real market for the shares, this is a pretty slim excuse).

However, at **the AGM** all legitimate questions have to be answered or provision has to be made for answering them in due course. The opportunity to air points that you would like satisfied should not be missed. Far too many shareholders of small to medium sized companies fail to exercise their rights in controlling management by subjecting them to the rigour of asking questions at the Annual General Meeting.

Chapter 24:

Predicting Results

---

*The risks and pitfalls
*Breaking the task down into little pieces
*Consistency between components of the forecast
*Checklists of factors to consider

Having analysed the accounts until you feel that you understand them thoroughly, the only task remaining may be to
make some tentative predictions about the future for the
company or business in which you are interested. This is
very much an 'optional extra' as far as analysing accounts is
concerned but it will almost certainly broaden your understanding of the business if you make a stab at forecasting
the coming year's results.

There may be crucial questions that you want to satisfy
yourself about: Will Company X be a suitable trading
partner? Will it grow as an investment? Can your investment in it continue to pay dividends?

However, you must never forget that profit prediction is a
game with few consistent winners and that any forecast will
be overtaken by real world events within a very short period
of time.

When I analysed company accounts for a living I used to
get a good proportion of my predictions right. (If I hadn't I
wouldn't have been employed for very long!) This was
because I knew the industry with which I was involved well,
I had a good grasp of the individual circumstances of the
companies I was looking at and I could de-construct a set of
accounts passably well.

But, if I am honest, the predictions I made looked better taken in the round than if you looked closely at the detail of any one component of the forecast. At the very detailed level, my predictions might well be seriously adrift. If I was lucky they were a sufficiently small part of the overall result not to make too much difference. (Sometimes though I was less lucky and the components of the forecast all went the wrong way at the same time!)

This would be true for all the people who were doing the same job as me in all the other competitive firms of brokers – simply because no-one has yet found a method of accurately predicting the pattern of events without uncertainty. And the further out that you try to predict the future, the more likely you are to fall flat on your face.

Looking ahead into the future may be a difficult task to embark on but don't be daunted by the apparent complexity of what you are trying to do. Like all the other tasks we have been through, if you cut it down into manageable pieces then, for a simple business, it should not prove too difficult. Having concluded the exercises of taking the accounts apart successfully, you now have all the requisite skills to build up a prediction of the trading pattern for the future.

If the business you are looking at appears to be complex with lots of divisions then the task can be cut down into manageable pieces by working out predictions for each individual division. There really is no difficulty then in making overall predictions for any size of business – because you can consider groups to be merely aggregations of single businesses and treat your predictions of their trading all in the same way.

To be thorough, any prediction about future trading must consider whether there will be a drain on cash or the generation of cash and what the consequential effect on interest charges will be. To be watertight, forecasts at a professional level should include forecasts of Sources and Uses of Funds and resulting Balance Sheets as well as Profit and Loss accounts. To be accurate the forecast must be internally consistent – all the parts must agree with each other. You could not normally have a forecast, for instance, that showed turnover increasing and profits rising without any change in Working Capital.

For most purposes a fully worked-through forecast for all the accounts components is likely to result in numerical overkill and prediction headaches that are not warranted by the purpose to which the forecasts will be put. You are predicting for your own purposes – not for the purposes of making investment predictions for others. The rigour required for giving advice to others is not what you need consider here – although you should, of course, make sure that your predictions are internally consistent between P&L, Balance Sheet and S&U.

How do you Start?

Well, in forecasting you are primarily concerned with performance in the market place – which means that you begin by looking at the trading results. And as with the process of taking the accounts apart, you start from the top and consider the way that the turnover may change.

The way that you do this is to look at the trend of the turnover line over the last few sets of accounts and consider the likely run in the next period. This will have to take into account the factors you will have already considered in going through the accounts, such as:

Is the market place expanding or contracting?

Is the business's share of that market place going up or down?

Is there any marked seasonality to the business's pattern of trading?

Have any new products been released which will affect the pattern of trading?

Are there any other special factors unique to the business which should be taken into account – such as takeovers or disposals just effected or about to happen?

Are there any price rises imminent in the company's trading policy?

What is the economic background going to be over the forecast period?

In looking at the trend of turnover it is very important that the half-yearly figures be used to try to form a pattern of trading over the next trading cycle. If you don't have the half-yearly pattern then you will have to concentrate on making yearly forecasts only.

You may find that this will lead to some inaccuracy beyond what might be expected in making half yearly forecasts and combining them, since there will inevitably be greater crudity in the assumptions that you can apply and you will be looking at a forecast that extends over a longer period of time. This means that there will be greater uncertainty about the conditions that the business will face over the forecast period. If you can, it is easier, and almost certainly more accurate, to forecast two separate, consecutive six month periods than to try to forecast a complete twelve-month at one go.

Use percentage changes first of all and see what numbers they throw up when you convert them back to indicate what happens to profit. Start with maybe a five per cent increase, if you think that the trends suggest an increase. If the numbers look ridiculous – just on the 'feel' of them – then have another go.

Usually, when turnover starts to fall, on the other hand, it goes down more than you might think, so if you think that the business is facing difficult market conditions you should probably start with a ten per cent drop.

Once you have had a go at forecasting the turnover then

you must look at the gross margin. Again, it's better if you can use two six-month sequences rather than go for the full year at one swoop. And again you must look at the run of the trading margin over a number of reporting periods to see if you can detect a trend. If you can detect something – then apply it. But don't do this unthinkingly. Ask yourself if there have been changes in the business which will mean that the trend that you have identified will be continued – or altered in some way. For instance:

Has new management been recruited?

Has the business made any published statements about what it intends to do in its market?

Have competitors said or done something significant?

Can any forthcoming changes in raw materials prices be covered by the business?

As well as these questions, ask yourself similar questions to those which you asked before about the conditions that the company is facing for turnover and try to work out what you think will happen to the percentage margin. Apply that to the turnover and then check it to see if it looks right in the context of what you believe market conditions to be. Margins tend to fall faster and harder than they rise, just in the same way that turnover usually falls faster than it goes up.

After the gross profit line (which you will remember takes into account only the cost of raw materials and the *direct* costs expended creating finished goods) you will have to think whether there is going to be any change in the cost of other inputs that will make a significant difference to the business. For instance:

Are staff numbers rising or falling?

Are premises costs increasing (are there more locations from which the business is trading?)

Are increased advertising costs going to affect the business?

And once you have completed this level of prediction, although you haven't finished with the P&L, you will have to think about cash flow. The next factor to forecast is the cost of borrowing for the business or the benefit gained from having money on deposit.

Here you will have to consider questions like:

Is the company expanding physically (and so spending more on Fixed Assets)?

Is its customer base expanding so that the cost of credit it has to offer will cause an outflow of funds?

Has a large chunk of the depreciation that was charged last year disappeared with the sale of that subsidiary that was also losing money?

The number of permutations of questions at this stage is huge. Here, the work that you have done in reading and analysing the accounts, press reports, industry reports and other background research will pay off. You will have to think around the business, using your own knowledge and benefiting from that which you have gained in analysing the accounts, to make sensible predictions for the future.

Once you have completed these stages you will have arrived at the prospective pre-tax position for the company. (You cannot, by definition, forecast Extraordinary or Exceptional charges). Then, if you want to, you can take things further and calculate the prospective earnings per share and P/E ratio (dividing your forecast profit after a 'notional tax charge' by the number of shares in issue and then the current share price by the earnings per share; see Appendix 6 for more details of how this is done).

Carrying Information as you Go Along

All through this exercise you should have been holding in your head the changes that you are contemplating will happen to the business during the forthcoming period, and making sure that you mentally allow for their effects on other parts of the forecasting process.

For instance I have already suggested that you must consider the effects on cash of an expansion in trade. This might mean that the business has to 'fund' its customers.

But it might also mean that stock levels go up, requiring still further funding. Or, conversely, it might mean that the company has to invest in better stock management practices, which should, in fact, reduce cash utilisation over time! If you feel it necessary to go on to calculate and forecast a Balance Sheet and S&U, then you MUST take these consequences into account in such a way that you can ascribe values to them. The touchy-feely method of saying 'up a bit' for that or 'down a bit' for this will not be adequate if you decide you need to adopt the rigorous approach of tying everything up with a full forecasting exercise.

Check and Re-check

Regardless of whether you choose the full forecasting exercise or the abbreviated method (without forecasting each of the components of the accounts individually), you must be sure that you look at your original forecasts again to see that you have indeed taken all these factors you can envisage into account – and, if necessary, go back and alter and re-alter until you feel that you have made sufficient allowance for the effects that you are considering.

Personally I do not recommend that you undertake a full forecasting exercise unless you have some prior, practical experience of accounting (in which case you probably aren't reading this book anyway!) since the benefit derived is unlikely to be worth the brain-pain suffered. For most purposes of a private-investment type, a back-of-the-envelope approach will probably be good enough given the uncertainties that will surround forecasts.

But if you want to, go ahead – and good for you!

Appendix 1

An Example of a Profit and Loss Account

Shown opposite the next page is a hybrid P&L constructed from a number of sources which shows some of the characteristics of both the Management accounts and the Statutory Accounts that have been discussed in the text.

One particularly noteworthy aspect of this P&L is that, in common with most sets of Management accounts and all Statutory Accounts formats, you will not find any reference in the P&L itself to **depreciation**. It is a convention of accounts' presentation that details of depreciation are contained among the Notes to the Financial Statements. There will be a section in the Notes which says something like, 'Operational Profit is stated after charging depreciation of £-, amortisation of intangible assets of £- and auditor's remuneration of £-'. (The exact wording will differ but should always contain references to depreciation and auditor's remuneration.) And there will also be a breakdown of depreciation against a Note to the fixed asset valuations in the Balance Sheet.

Statutory Accounts will not have the variance to budget indications, of course, since this is strictly management information; nor will they contain any calculations of margins.

The format of Management accounts is left to the discretion of the managers of a business and is not prescribed by law or accounting standards (Financial Reporting Standards, to give them their full name), as is the format of Statutory Accounts. On this P&L I have followed the accounting convention of using brackets round negative (deductible) figures rather than minus signs.

You will also see that this example P&L indicates that the managers of the business are budgeting for a loss in the current period and that the performance of the company to date is roughly twice as bad as that for which they had originally budgeted. While they have done what they can to contain costs (variable and fixed costs are both down below budget) and finance costs have been reduced below expectations in the current period, the business is still suffering badly from the effects of reduced turnover and the worst of this is being felt in export markets. The actual gross margin, while above budgeted levels for the most recently reported period, is below the year-to-date actual – which suggests that there might have been a sudden fall in trading activity shortly into the year after a reasonably good start.

It is also possible to speculate from the pattern of figures given that the worst may be over, since the figures for the most recently reported period are not as bad as the year-to-date results. However, it would require more sets of numbers – either from preceding periods or from succeeding ones (and preferably both) – before you could be certain about this.

Suggestions like these about the pattern of trading should only be conjectural and not held too firmly until you can validate your suspicions with firmer evidence. But they do provide a useful starting point to look for trends in the accounts.

Example Profit & Loss Account

	Current month			Year to date		
	Actual £000	Budgeted £000	Variance	Actual £000	Budgeted £000	Variance
Gross Sales						
UK	345,930	459,100	-24%	1,754,938	2,546,900	-31%
Export	157,365	225,500	-30%	1,235,146	2,038,300	-39%
Cost of Sales	(372,620)	(521,200)	-20%	(2,183,707)	(3,492,000)	-26%
Gross Profit	130,675	163,400		806,377	1,093,200	
Gross Margin	26%	24%		27%	24%	
Variable Overheads	(34,305)	(48,300)	-29%	(208,080)	(315,000)	-34%
Fixed Overheads	(67,091)	(79,870)	-16%	(634,243)	(714,272)	-11%
Operating Profit	29,279	35,230	-17%	(35,946)	63,928	-156%
Finance Costs	(17,674)	(22,100)		(137,326)	(161,800)	
Profit before Tax	11,605	13,130	-12%	(173,272)	(97,872)	-77%

Appendix 2

An Example of a Balance Sheet

The example of a Balance Sheet which follows on pages 168/9 shows most of the characteristics of layout and that have been discussed in the chapters on Balance Sheets. Each of the categories and headings would be accompanied by a numbered note, if the accounts were real, which would explain in much greater detail the composition of the individual items displayed.

There are a number of things that can be deduced from this Balance Sheet without delving any further than the information shown.

It shows a company with a robust asset base with lots of fixed assets (so the chances are that it is in some form of manufacturing activity). It looks as if it has been acquisitive in the past or maybe that it has a large number of valuable brands, or perhaps patent rights that are extremely valuable (the intangible assets). Or, possibly, a combination of all three.

It looks as if it made a disposal in the last year reported on, since the share of joint venture assets and liabilities both declined. While stockholdings went up, the debtors list and the amount of cash stayed broadly the same, so it looks as if maybe the company took advantage of credit from suppliers to pay for the increase in stock. But it could have raised extra loans in the short term to pay off some of the longer term debt in its Balance Sheet, since short-term debt and long-term debt both changed by about the same amounts. The company is not heavily geared at about 33% of total capital employed (total debt less cash as a proportion of total capital employed).

166

There was obviously a small issue of shares during the year since the called-up share capital increased by a small amount and the share premium account also went up very slightly. Possibly shares were issued as part payment for an acquisition.

You will also see that there are two places in this Balance Sheet where small 'investments' are identified. The first of these – of **£0.5**m under **Fixed Assets** – refers to an investment in subsidiary companies. The second – of **£0.1**m under **Current Assets** – is a trace of an investment in the more casual, personal sense of the word and probably indicates where the company has 'parked' some spare cash – perhaps in government securities.

An Example of a Balance Sheet

Consolidated Balance Sheet

	as at 31/12/year £m		as at 31/12/previous year £m	
Fixed Assets				
Intangible assets		62.2		39.1
Tangible assets		136.5		133
Investments in joint ventures				
share of gross assets	42.6		48.7	
share of gross liabilities	(40.4)		(45.9)	
share of goodwill	1.7		1.8	
Investment		3.9		4.6
		0.5		0.5
		203.1		177.2
Current Assets				
Stocks		89.1		77
Debtors amount falling due within 1 year		127.6		126.1
Investments		0.1		0.9
Cash at bank and in hand		35.2		32.8
		252		236.8

Current Liabilities			
Creditors: amounts falling due within 1 year			
borrowings	(52.5)		(26.6)
other creditors	(115.8)		(110.9)
		(168.3)	(137.5)
Net Current Assets		83.7	99.3
Total Assets Less Current Liabilities		286.8	276.5
Creditors			
amounts falling due after 1 year			
borrowings	(46.3)		(69.8)
other creditors	(3.4)		(1.9)
		(49.7)	(71.7)
Provisions for Liabilities and Charges		(15.2)	(14.3)
Net Assets [employed]		221.9	190.5
Capital and Reserves including non-equity interests			
Called-up Share Capital	24.7		24.6
Share Premium Account	53.7		52.6
Revaluation Reserve	1.7		1.7
Other Reserve	0.6		0.3
Profit and Loss Account	140.8		111.1
		221.5	190.3
Minority equity interest		0.4	0.2
Shareholders' Funds		221.9	190.5

Appendix 3

An Example of a Sources and Uses of Funds Statement

The table shows a Sources and Uses of Funds statement from an imaginary company. It follows the format that is described in the text at Chapters 13 and 22. This is not a rigid or definitive format and other orders of listing of the individual items may be used according to the preferences of the compiler of the accounts.

Quite a lot can be revealed by only a simple dissection of the S&U without any great effort. For instance:

Profits in the most recent year have gone up substantially. Could the acquisition of the large subsidiary (for the purchase of which the company raised cash from the issue of shares) have accounted for this? Interest on the large sums raised – which were also used to pay down the overdraft – might have also contributed to this improvement.

A small subsidiary was sold in the year and a very large amount spent on purchasing Fixed Assets (apart from the subsidiary itself). Could these two things indicate a re-positioning of the business when coupled with the increase in profits and the expansion in working capital that has taken place (mostly down to the funding of the company's customers apparently, indicated by the expansion in the debtors' list)?

The capital expenditure and the acquisition of the subsidiary have left the business without the reserves of cash brought about by the proceeds of the share issue – but with a much reduced (possibly eliminated) overdraft. What will happen to cash requirements next year? Might the

XYZ Manufacturing Ltd

	Current year **£**	Previous year £
Sources of funds		
Profit before tax	**560,000**	450,000
Exceptional items	**0**	(125,000)
Depreciation	**300,000**	275,000
Disposal of fixed assets	**0**	10,000
Sale of subsidiary	**50,000**	0
Shares issued	**0**	750,000
Total Sources	**910,000**	1,360,000
Use of funds		
Increase (decrease) in stock	**25,000**	5,000
(Increase) decrease in creditors	**(25,000)**	5,000
Increase (decrease) in debtors	**65,000**	5,000
Purchase of fixed assets	**500,000**	50,000
Tax paid	**125,000**	85,000
Dividends paid	**10,000**	10,000
Purchase of subsidiaries	**1,250,000**	0
Total Uses	**1,950,000**	160,000
Net Inflow/Outflow	**(1,040,000)**	1,200,000
Funded by		
Change in overdraft	**0**	(100,000)
Change in long term loans	**0**	0
Change in cash holdings	**(1,040,000)**	1,100,000

expanded creditors' list have to be paid off, absorbing cash? Could the debtors' list be reduced, generating cash? Could another share issue be made? Will shareholders be satisfied with the continuation of comparatively modest dividend payments in relation to the size of recent pre-tax profits?

Appendix 4

Current Cost Accounting: FIFO versus LIFO

Earlier on we talked about the various methods of recording stock and the effect that these might have on calculated profits. This appendix illustrates the effect, on profit, of taking into account inflation in the cost of raw materials.

The Cost of Sales is the P&L item that links directly into the Balance Sheet via the stock line. It is this link between the two that makes the valuation of stock so crucially important for the calculation of profits – since the amount of stock used in achieving profit involves the difference between the value of stock held at the beginning of the year and the value of that held at the end of the year. It follows that the way that stock is valued at the end of the year, or, in times of high inflation, *throughout* the year, will directly impact profitability.

Most of the time, during periods of stable prices, the valuation of stock at the year end is quite simple – the accounting concept of prudence requires that the lower of the price at which each item was purchased or their current market value is taken. If this is the case then the prices of raw materials for costing purposes can be assumed to be more or less constant.

However, in times of inflation (or, theoretically, of deflation) this measure can go seriously awry, since prices can be changing so fast that year end values can be very different from current (replacement) values. Unless manufacturers are alert and able to raise prices constantly, the prices being charged to eventual customers will reflect yesterday's raw material prices rather then the ones which are currently obtaining in the market.

Since a manufacturer will have to pay the inflated replacement price for replenishing his stocks, it does not take too much technical ability to see that this can lead to very serious consequences as far as profitability and cash flow are concerned. Hence the importance of 'inflation accounting'.

To overcome this problem, Management accountants developed the LIFO stock costing system to use in place of the more traditional FIFO. LIFO stands for 'Last In First Out' while FIFO stands for 'First In First Out'. (To reassure the nervous or confused, the terminology only applies to the *prices* at which goods came into inventory and *not* the physical removal from stock of items needed in manufacture – since this would offend good manufacturing practice).

Chapter 18 on P&L Costs and Mischief deals with the theoretical application of the system, so here I will confine further description to a simple practical example which should make the operation of the principle clear.

Three friends, all Brownies – Abigail, Anna and Kathleen, all aged 9 – make decorated biscuits, which they sell at 10p each to raise funds for the local Brownie pack . They have a big tin of biscuits in the kitchen of Kathleen's home to which they contribute communally, filling the tin – and taking stock from it – on a random basis when they get together every few days to ice the biscuits, which they do with icing provided free by their mothers.

They decide to count the contents of the tin each week-end to check how many they have been using (since they believe that Kathleen's brother, Philip, may be eating some of their stock) and to work out how much they have spent on the biscuits, so that they will know what the profit is.

At the start of the first week there are exactly thirty biscuits in the tin on the Monday morning, which had been bought by Kathleen at 55p a packet (10 biscuits). Kathleen buys another two packets during the week (20 biscuits) on Tuesday and Friday; Anna buys a packet on Wednesday; and

Abigail buys two packets (20 biscuits), both on Saturday, just before they have their big weekend icing session. At the end of the week, on Sunday night, they all sit down around Kathleen's kitchen table and count the biscuits remaining in the tin.

Kathleen gets a piece of paper and records the calculation as follows:

Biscuits at start of week:	30
Biscuits at end of week:	10
Biscuits added during week:	50 (2 × 10; plus 1 × 10; plus 2 × 10)
Biscuits decorated and sold during week:	70 (30 to start plus 50 added *less* 10 remaining)

'Well,' says Kathleen, '*that* agrees with what I think we made. But it's a lot of biscuits. And it must have cost us a fortune.'

'I was paying 75p a packet,' says Abigail. 'And the price had gone up and I paid 60p at the Co-op,' says Kathleen. 'And I paid 70p at the corner shop,' says Anna.

'Well, we'd better try to work out how much it cost,' says Kathleen and they spend the next hour arguing how much the stock of remaining biscuits cost and what the profit earned so far was.

Let's assume that the girls' appreciation of accounts is marginally more sophisticated than that of ordinary 9 year old Brownies.

Anna says that they should adopt a FIFO basis for measuring the cost of what they have used. Abigail agrees and they start to calculate their costs and profits. The argument would run like this: what came in first, went out first. So, of the 70 biscuits used, the first 30 were from original stock; then came Kathleen's first top up 10; then Anna's 10; and then Kathleen's second packet of 10; following these came a packet from Abigail and the 10 left were the remainder from her purchase of two packets. So the value of the stock of biscuits left over is simple. It is equal to the price Abigail paid – 1 pack (10 biscuits) at 75p per pack.

It follows from this FIFO basis that the overall cost of the biscuits decorated for sale was equal to (3 × 55p) + (60p) + (70p) + (60p) + (75p); or £4.30.

But Kathleen is unhappy about this. 'No girls,' she says. 'That doesn't look right to me. I think we have got it wrong. Our stock cost us more as we went along so the profits will be affected. I suggest that we use the LIFO method.'

To humour Kathleen, Abigail and Anna agree to recast the numbers. In this case the last-bought biscuits are used first.

So the entire purchase bought by Abigail on Saturday went, as did all of Anna's 10 biscuits and both top-up packets of 10 bought by Kathleen, as well as 20 (two packets) of the original stock at the beginning of the week (bought by Kathleen some time earlier).

The remaining ten biscuits are therefore all part of the original lot bought at 55p per packet or 5½p each.

The cost of the biscuits sold is now:

(2 × 75p – from Abigail's Saturday purchase) + (70p – from Anna) + (2 × 60p from Kathleen's purchases during the week and 2 × 55p – from the original stock bought by Kathleen before the price went up); or £4.50, an increase of 4.7% in their costs.

The effect on the profitability of the girls' efforts was plain.

Using the FIFO method they made a profit of: £7 (70 biscuits × 10p each) *less* £4.30 for the cost of the biscuits = £2.70.

Using the LIFO method they made a profit of: £7 *less* £4.50 = £2.50 – a reduction of 7.4% in their reported profits over the FIFO method. This is because they had to pay out more for their stock as they went along and so the 'mixed' cost of the stock consumed was higher than it would have been using only the cheapest-priced stock. If the girls were decorating as a business and really did have to pay taxes on their profits, then the effect would be even plainer. They would have to pay out more in tax if they used FIFO.

Apart from adopting a tactic of buying everything from the Co-op where Kathleen shops, the friends may well have to increase their prices to 11p per biscuit to match or better their contribution to Brownie funds if the rise in the price of the biscuit raw materials continues. If they bought all their raw materials at the place where Abigail shops but could not raise their prices, they might eventually find that a continuing rise in raw materials would eliminate their profits!

To summarise, it should be fairly clear that the effect of using LIFO is to depress earnings through raising the value of the Cost of Sales line, and to inflate the year-end stock position by taking the highest value of raw materials as the guide multiplier for all the quantities involved. In times of high inflation these effects equate to real world conditions more closely than the FIFO basis of calculation.

As Kathleen went on to explain to Abigail and Anna:

'If we were doing this as a business then we should adopt LIFO to reflect the fact that our stock value is altering. That way we would have to pay less taxes. That would result from our profits being less because our Cost of Sales would be more. Another way would be to raise our prices in line with the increase in our raw material costs. Then, as we sold out our older raw materials, our earnings would get a further boost.'

Anna and Abigail nod in agreement and Abigail takes a bite out of one of the biscuits they have just decorated.

'I like the green icing best,' says Abigail. Kathleen rolls her eyes and props her chin on her hands.

Appendix 5

The PLC Cash Flow Statement

The PLC Cash Flow Statement is essentially the same as the S&U but starts off from a slightly different position and makes one or two further minor changes in style to accommodate international accounting rules. Its principle difference in format is that it 'mixes up' inflows and outflows rather than separating them out into individual boxes.

So, the cashflow statement of a PLC starts off (usually in a note marked against the Net Cash Inflow – which is the first item listed) with the cash generated from operational activities – which is operating profit as we have previously defined it:

To this it adds back the depreciation; in the same way as the S&U;

And then restores the amortisation of goodwill and intangibles (think of this as being like depreciation);

Next it will add any notional loss on disposal of Fixed Assets (or take off any notional profit) in order to 'equalise' the effect of depreciation and avoid double counting;

Then it does the same for current investments; taking off any gains or adding back losses that have been recorded;

It also makes provision for liabilities and charges (obviously a negative);

And takes into account gains and losses on foreign exchange (which can go either way);

Now it will make allowance for the cost of any long-term incentives offered to staff;

Take off any increase in stocks;

Add the decrease (or take off the increase) in debtors – and

178

the sum of all these calculations is then what you see on the Cash Flow Statement at the top line as '**Net Cash Inflow**'.

To this are then added returns on investments (only those taken in the form of dividends or interest payments since actual investment and realised gains and losses are dealt with elsewhere).

Costs of servicing borrowings and the amounts paid out in taxation are taken off (*not* VAT which, to remind you, is an in-and-out and hence neutral consideration).

Any capital expenditure undertaken is shown and allowance is made for the costs or proceeds of any acquisitions and disposals.

The cost of equity dividends paid out to shareholders is deducted.

The 'management of liquid resources' – which means utilisation of spare cash to buy or sell investments and the net purchase (or sale) of short-term deposits – comes next (plus or minus).

Finally, the effects of financing – increased or decreased borrowing are taken into account.

At the bottom of all this comes the key line, usually entitled **Increase / (Decrease) in cash**, which displays the overall result of the inflows and outflows taken together.

This Cashflow Statement is always accompanied by two more, smaller ones. The first of these, the **Statement of Recognised Gains & Losses**, follows further below. The second one reconciles the (Decrease)/Increase in cash identified to the actual movements in the components of the debt that the company may have. Not surprisingly this second table (which may be consigned to the Notes to the Financial Statements) usually goes by the catchy name of '**Reconciliation of Net Cash Flow to Movement in Net Debt**'.

The Statement of Recognised Gains and Losses

Closely allied to the PLC Cash Flow Statement is the Statement of Recognised Gains and Losses. You won't find this category of information in the accounts of companies that have no listing since it is solely a requirement of the Stock Exchange that it be included in the information provided to shareholders.

Like the Cash Flow Statement, the Statement of Recognised Gains and Losses takes pieces from both the Balance Sheet and the P&L to synthesise further information. Its purpose is to show the changes in shareholders' funds that actually arose from trading activity. So it strips out of the amounts added to shareholders' funds anything resulting from issues of shares or goodwill changes.

It does take into account any changes in valuations of assets, though, and any currency gains or losses. This seems rather confusing at first, until you realise that the purpose of this section of the accounts of listed companies is to highlight changes to shareholders' funds and lay bare the underlying reasons for these changes. If it did not include such information then it would not be fulfilling its purpose!

In truth, the Statement of Recognised Gains and Losses does not contribute much to the armoury of tools that the analyst employs since it does not provide any original information that was not previously disclosed. (Although, to be fair, the same could be said of the S&U, I suppose, since it is quite possible to construct an S&U from first principles using a P&L and a Balance Sheet.) However, it does make things clearer to an outsider and expands the amount of available information – particularly for instance about currency transactions – which can save time in rooting through the Notes to the Accounts.

Appendix 6

Professional Analysts' Techniques: The P/E ratio and others

The professional investment community has developed a number of established measures which it uses to evaluate the worth of investing in a business and making an estimate of a share price's prospects. This is a crucial element of the next stage of the evaluating process. But to use their measures we have to dip into the world – and the jargon – of professional investors for a moment.

The P/E Ratio – What it is

The first P&L-based measure of whether the shares of a business are worth investing in – which you have already come across briefly – is the P/E ratio, the Price Earnings ratio. Since we are talking about measures developed by professional investors, we are talking primarily about investing in shares that are probably *already traded* on a stock exchange. However, it can also be used in some other circumstances – it might crop up in probate work for instance. The P/E ratio is probably the sturdiest comparative measure between two businesses.

Definition:

The 'historic' **P/E ratio** is the current price of the share in question divided by the last reported annual earnings-per-share. The earnings per share are calculated by dividing the amount of post-tax profit by the number of shares in issue (or fully adjusted for any forthcoming changes in the share capital structure, in which case they are known as the 'fully adjusted eps'). The result is a relative measure of the costliness of different shares. The 'prospective P/E' is an estimate of the P/E using forecast profits.

The share price used in the calculation need not be publicly quoted but can be the price of shares in a private company which someone has asked to buy or sell. If this is the case, the share price quoted will usually be the last price at which a sale was effected.

What it Does

The P/E ratio is used to give an assessment of the value of a share in relation to others. It demonstrates a sort of characteristic that might be called 'investment potential' or 'investment attractiveness'.

Generally speaking, historical P/Es are of less interest to professional analysts than the prospects for movements in the share price. These are mostly governed by the relative attractiveness of one share compared with another.

For instance, let's suppose shares in XYZ Manufacturing plc have a current price of 600p (share prices are usually quoted in pence) and that there are 6 million shares in issue. With predicted profits after tax of £6 million, XYZ will then have prospective earnings of 100p per share (the use of the word prospective always indicates that the number is based on the predictions made by an analyst) . That would give it a prospective P/E of 6 – the current 600p (price) divided by 100p (earnings).

If the last reported P/E of XYZ (based on last year's results) was, say, 12 (indicative of an eps then of 50p) and the P/E of a competitor share of equivalent quality – let's call it ABC Manufacturing plc – already has a *prospective* P/E of 13, then our imaginary XYZ company would be rated a 'buy' by professional analysts because:

1)   It would take fewer years for its earnings to achieve the current share price than a year earlier, so the relative cost of buying the shares has fallen; and

2)   A similar business – ABC Manufacturing plc – already has a prospective P/E ratio that is over twice as high as XYZ's prospective P/E.

However, XYZ's share price might not move up at once even though it now appears to be cheaper than ABC's. This is because the decision whether to buy a share is usually not linked solely to the price.

Different investors may have different requirements of their investments, sliding up and down the risk/reward curve according to whether they value high rewards above security. For instance, some investors may want the prospect of fairly constant income from their investments, coupled with the chance of modest growth; some might prefer growth to income; some might want the gamble of very high growth and are willing to give up income, and possibly risk losing their investments entirely, to get it. Investors might rate XYZ's attractiveness more lowly than ABC's for a whole variety of reasons.

Dividend Yield

To pick the right shares for their different aspirations, analysts/investors will also take into account the **Dividend Yield** of the shares (the amount of gross dividend per share paid out by the company, divided by its share price) and the **'quality' of the earnings**, among other factors.

The Dividend Yield also has to be considered in comparison with those of other companies. Too high a Dividend Yield (in comparison with the rest of the market) cannot be sustained for long and too high a yield is probably telling you something about other people's estimation of the worth of the company involved.

On the other hand a low yield may suggest that the share price is currently over-valued and could be riding for a fall.

Or, conversely, it could mean that the company is very highly rated and regarded as a growth stock because investors are less concerned with dividends than the growth that the company can sustain by reinvesting its profits into a developing market. Judicious use has to be made of all the available information in reaching such conclusions.

Uncovered dividends – where there are insufficient profits to pay for the dividend out of the profits after tax of the year just finished – are unlikely to be sustained for long and are usually a warning of a dividend about to be cut if profits cannot be raised.

Quality of Earnings

This other factor which plays upon the attractiveness of an investment in a company – quality of earnings – depends upon subjective considerations rather than any arithmetic relationship. It cannot be taught or described in the same way as any quantitative method.

For instance, the quality of the earnings of a major supermarket chain would probably be considered to be higher than that of a youngish company developing computer software games. The supermarket's stream of income is large, probably reasonably consistent and drawn from a spread of products. The software developer's may also be large but is probably also dependent upon demand for its products from a fickle market-place and is therefore less well tested over time than that of the supermarket. The amount of earnings – sheer size – is not the factor under consideration here.

There are other intangibles such as:

a)   the reliance that can be placed on the continuation of the stream of income;
b)   investors' perceptions about the quality of the business's managers;
c)   the range of products from which the income stream derives.

And these things can change. Marks and Spencer used to be perceived as having higher quality earnings than Sainsbury's, which, in turn, had higher quality earnings than Tesco; most analysts would probably have up-ended that ordering by the end of the nineteen-nineties. But opinions will differ between analysts. This is what, after all, creates a market place – differences in perception about the value of goods and services.

Appendix 7

Further Reading

Readers who find that they would like to know more about specific details of accounts will find many texts available at a variety of levels of sophistication. The following texts are easily understood and cover a variety of topics that have been touched on this book:

Creative Accounting, Ian Griffiths, published by Sidgwick and Jackson, 1986.

Select Winning Stocks, Richard Loth, published by Dearborn (USA), 1999.

Interpreting Company Reports and Accounts, Holmes and Sugden, published by Woodhead Faulkner (various editions; frequently up-dated; the standard introductory text for analysts).

Manias, Panics and Crashes, Charles Kindleberger, Wiley, 1996.

The Art of Speculation, Philip L Carret, (1930) re-issued by Wiley, 1997.

Sources of accounts' information – Companies' House Documents
Apply to:

The Registrar, Companies' House, Crown Way, Cardiff CF14 4UZ

HemScott Guides are published by

HS Financial Publishing Ltd., 26-31 Whiskin Street, London EC1R 0JD

Index